The
Practical Grammar Handbook
for College Writers

The
Practical Grammar Handbook
for College Writers

Third Edition

Marian Anders

CAROLINA ACADEMIC PRESS
Durham, North Carolina

Library of Congress Cataloging-in-Publication Data

Names: Anders, Marian, author.
Title: The practical grammar handbook for college writers / Marian Anders.
Description: Third edition. | Durham, North Carolina : Carolina Academic
  Press, 2017. | Includes bibliographical references and index.
Identifiers: LCCN 2017025427 | ISBN 9781531005436 (alk. paper)
Subjects: LCSH: English language--Grammar. | English language--Rhetoric. |
  Report writing.
Classification: LCC PE1112 .A54 2017 | DDC 428.2--dc23
LC record available at https://lccn.loc.gov/2017025427

Carolina Academic Press, LLC
700 Kent Street
Durham, NC 27701
Telephone (919) 489-7486
Fax (919) 493-5668
www.cap-press.com

Printed in the United States of America

Contents

Contents

Contents

Contents

Contents

Contents

Contents

Contents

Contents

Introduction

As a student, I always enjoyed English, but I never understood grammar. I had a natural talent for language and writing, so I got good grades on my papers without knowing what I was doing.

I began learning grammar when I was working on my Master's degree in English at Florida State University. When I became a teacher and saw my students getting frustrated by the traditional approach to learning grammar, I developed a more practical approach which presents the material step-by-step and provides a variety of tricks for students to use.

I have taught English grammar, composition, and literature to college freshmen and sophomores for over twenty years, and the methods presented in this handbook work for all kinds of students, those who love writing and those who find it difficult. These methods work because they are based on logic rather than intuition or memorization.

My students have told me, "I always hated English, but this isn't too bad," and "I never understood grammar before, but this method makes it easy." *The Practical Grammar Handbook for College Writers* focuses on what you need to know and explains everything quickly and clearly. Grammar may never be your favorite subject, but it doesn't have to be a mystery or a misery.

—Marian Anders

About the Author

Marian Anders earned a Master of Arts degree in English from Florida State University. She has over twenty-five years' experience teaching all levels of grammar and composition, from basic skills developmental to advanced college grammar. She teaches English at Alamance Community College in Graham, North Carolina.

Acknowledgments

I offer my thanks to the many English teachers I have had the privilege of working with over the years. By sharing ideas and supporting each other, we have all become better teachers. I especially thank Jeannie Murphy, my friend and mentor from Pierce College who taught me the intricacies of traditional grammar, and Nancy Bolle, also from Pierce College, who was a supportive friend when I was a new teacher.

Abundant thanks also to my family for their invaluable support.

This book is dedicated to all my students—past, present, and future.

The
Practical Grammar Handbook
for College Writers

Chapter One

✧

Verbs and Subjects

Most people have learned to find the subject of a sentence by asking, "What is the sentence about?" To find the verb, most people have been told, "Look for an action word." Sometimes that method works, but often it doesn't.

> She enjoys baking brownies.

What is this sentence about? Most people would say *brownies*. What is the action word? Most people would say *baking*. But the subject of this sentence is not *brownies*; it's *she*. And the verb is not *baking;* it's *enjoys*.

In this chapter you will learn to find the verb first and then the subject by using a method that always works.

Take your time on this chapter because everything you need to know about grammar builds on your ability to find the verb and the subject.

Finding Verbs

Most people were taught to find the verb in a sentence by looking for the action word. Sometimes that method works, but other times it doesn't. The **time change** method is much easier to use, and it always works.

Change the time of the sentence by saying *yesterday, every day,* and *tomorrow* at the beginning of the sentence. When you change the time of the sentence, the verb will change automatically.

Listen for the word that changes when you change the time. That word is the verb.

> *Yesterday* Steve **ATE** a pizza. (past)
> *Every day* Steve **EATS** a pizza. (present)
> *Tomorrow* Steve **WILL EAT** a pizza. (future)

> *Yesterday* Jill **BOUGHT** a new pair of shoes.
> *Every day* Jill **BUYS** a new pair of shoes.
> *Tomorrow* Jill **WILL BUY** a new pair of shoes.

Try these sentences on your own and then check your answers below.

> My dog bites the English teacher.
> *Yesterday* My dog . . .
> *Every day* My dog . . .
> *Tomorrow* My dog . . .

Here are the answers:

> *Yesterday* My dog **BIT** the English teacher.
> *Every day* My dog bites the English teacher. (no change)
> *Tomorrow* My dog **WILL BITE** the English teacher.

In the *every day* sentence, nothing changed because the original sentence was already in the present. The verb changes when you change the time. The word *bites* changed, so *bites* is the verb.

Now try this one and check your answers below:

> My brother Charlie got a flat tire.
> *Yesterday* My brother Charlie . . .
> *Every day* My brother Charlie . . .
> *Tomorrow* My brother Charlie . . .

Here are the answers:

> *Yesterday* My brother Charlie got a flat tire. (no change)
> *Every day* My brother Charlie **GETS** a flat tire.
> *Tomorrow* My brother Charlie **WILL GET** a flat tire.

This time the *yesterday* sentence didn't change because the original sentence was already in the past. The word *got* changed, so *got* is the verb.

When you change the time to find the verb, use all three time words; the verb will change with two of them.

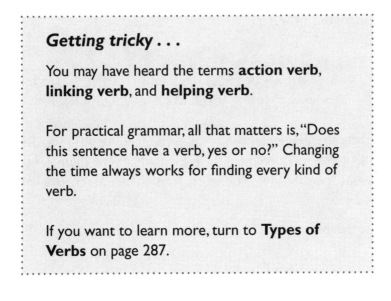

Getting tricky . . .

You may have heard the terms **action verb**, **linking verb**, and **helping verb**.

For practical grammar, all that matters is, "Does this sentence have a verb, yes or no?" Changing the time always works for finding every kind of verb.

If you want to learn more, turn to **Types of Verbs** on page 287.

Let's try some tricky sentences. Remember, don't look for the verb. Listen for the word that changes.

> Jackie loves playing volleyball.
> *Yesterday* Jackie **LOVED** playing volleyball.
> *Every day* Jackie loves playing volleyball.
> *Tomorrow* Jackie **WILL LOVE** playing volleyball.

The word that changed is *loves*, so *loves* is the verb.

Are you surprised that *playing* wasn't the verb? *Playing* looks like an action word, but it did not change when we changed the time. The real verb will always change.

> **Getting tricky . . .**
>
> If **playing** isn't the verb, what is it?
>
> **Playing** is a **direct object**. See page 296 for an explanation of direct objects.

Try finding the verb in these sentences and then check your answers below:

> Susan enjoyed jogging in the park.
> *Yesterday* Susan . . .
> *Every day* Susan . . .
> *Tomorrow* Susan . . .
>
> Mark wants to win the trophy.
> *Yesterday* Mark . . .
> *Every day* Mark . . .
> *Tomorrow* Mark . . .

Here are the answers:

> Susan enjoyed jogging in the park.
> *Yesterday* Susan enjoyed jogging in the park.
> *Every day* Susan **ENJOYS** jogging in the park.
> *Tomorrow* Susan **WILL ENJOY** jogging in the park.

The verb is the word that changed: *enjoyed*. Why isn't *jogging* the verb? *Jogging* didn't change when we changed the time.

> Mark wants to win the race.
> *Yesterday* Mark **WANTED** to win the race.
> *Every day* Mark wants to win the race.
> *Tomorrow* Mark **WILL WANT** to win the race.

The verb is the word that changed: *wants*. Why isn't *win* the verb? *Win* didn't change when we changed the time.

The verb is always the word that changes.

Getting tricky . . .

If **jogging** and **win** aren't verbs, what are they?

Jogging and **to win** are both **direct objects**.

See page 296 for an explanation of direct objects.

Jogging is also a **gerund**, explained on page 291.

To win is also an **infinitive** explained on page 291.

Sentences with More than One Verb

A sentence can have more than one verb. When you change the time, all the verbs in the sentence will change.

> The garden will look beautiful and smell heavenly.
>
> *Yesterday* The garden **LOOKED** beautiful and **SMELLED** heavenly.
>
> *Every day* The garden **LOOKS** beautiful and **SMELLS** heavenly.

If the sentence is long, it can be useful to say the time word again in the middle.

> Gloria washed the dishes, and Bob dried them.
>
> *Every day* Gloria **WASHES** the dishes, and *every day* Bob **DRIES** them.
>
> *Tomorrow* Gloria **WILL WASH** the dishes, and *tomorrow* Bob **WILL DRY** them.

Exercise 1.1 Finding Verbs

Say *yesterday, every day,* and *tomorrow* at the beginning of each sentence and listen for the words that change. Some sentences have one verb, and others have two. Mark the verbs with a <u>double</u> <u>underline</u>.

Check your answers on page 313.

1. My neighbor George loves gardening.

2. Every weekend he works in his yard.

3. George went on-line and ordered six apple trees.

4. The trees came in the mail in a large cardboard box; they were only three feet tall.

5. George sweated profusely as he dug six holes in his yard.

6. Blisters stung his hands, yet he continued working.

7. Then he shoveled compost into each hole.

8. After planting the trees, George firmed the soil around their roots.

9. Soon the little trees will bloom, and the blossoms will look so pretty.

10. In only four years, George will harvest his first apples.

Exercise 1.2 Finding Verbs

Say *yesterday, every day,* and *tomorrow* at the beginning of each sentence and listen for the words that change. Some sentences have one verb, and others have two. Mark the verbs with a double underline.

Check your answers on page 314.

1. Video games are a multi-billion dollar industry.

2. Many people think that *Pong* was the first video game.

3. *Pong* comes from the game of table tennis; in *Pong* players slide the paddles back and forth to hit the ball.

4. Although *Pong* was not the first video game, its success took the video game industry mainstream.

5. Earlier video games included *Spacewar* and *Chase; Chase* was the first video game for television.

6. Some teachers use computer games to teach their students.

7. Programs allow students to play a game after they master a new concept.

8. Typing programs include games to improve typing speed.

9. Some museums use video games as part of their displays such as the stock trading simulation game at the Chicago Board of Trade Museum.

10. After finishing these sentences, you will reward your-self and play your favorite video game.

Finding Subjects

When you analyze a sentence, always find the verb first. Then you can find the subject by asking yourself, "Who or what performed the verb?"

Janisa baked a peach pie.

Tomorrow Janisa **WILL BAKE** a peach pie.

Every day Janisa **BAKES** a peach pie.

The verb is *baked*. To find the subject, ask yourself, "Who or what baked a peach pie?"

The answer, of course, is *Janisa*. Mark subjects with a <u>single underline</u>.

<u>Janisa</u> <u>baked</u> a peach pie.

Were you tempted to mark *pie* as the subject? Ask yourself, "Did the pie bake anything?" No, Janisa baked it, so the subject is <u>*Janisa*</u>.

Getting tricky . . .

If **pie** isn't the subject, what is it?

Pie is a **direct object**. See page 296.

In most sentences, the subject comes before the verb. The subject can come after the verb, but that doesn't happen too often.

Getting tricky . . .

For examples of sentences in which the subject comes after the verb, see pages 292–296.

Sentences with More than One Subject

Katie and Jake <u>swim</u> at the YMCA.

The verb is *swim*. To find the subject, ask yourself, "Who or what swims at the YMCA?" Katie and Jake both swim. They are two subjects sharing one verb, so underline both names:

<u>Katie</u> and <u>Jake</u> <u>swim</u> at the YMCA.

A sentence can have several verbs and several subjects.

> Gloria <u>washed</u> the dishes, and Bob <u>dried</u> them.

Ask the subject question for each verb. "Who or what washed the dishes?" *Gloria* washed the dishes. "Who or what dried them?" *Bob* dried them.

Underline both subjects:

> <u>Gloria</u> <u>washed</u> the dishes, and <u>Bob</u> <u>dried</u> them.

Here's a harder one:

> After he <u>mowed</u> the lawn, Andre <u>took</u> a shower, and then he <u>watched</u> TV.

Ask the subject question for each verb, and remember that the subject will usually come before its verb. "Who or what mowed the lawn?" *He* mowed the lawn. "Who or what took a shower? *Andre* took a shower. "Who or what watched tv?" *He* watched TV.

Underline all the subjects:

> After <u>he</u> <u>mowed</u> the lawn, <u>Andre</u> <u>took</u> a shower, and then <u>he</u> <u>watched</u> TV.

> **Getting tricky . . .**
>
> The subject of the sentence will either be a **noun** or **pronoun**. For an explanation of nouns and pronouns, see page 305.

One-Word Subjects

Usually it's best to underline just one word for each subject.

My brother <u>is</u> a scuba instructor.

"Who or what is a scuba instructor?" *My brother.*

If you want to underline only one word, which word would you choose? *Brother* is a better choice than *my.*

My <u>brother</u> <u>is</u> a scuba instructor.

Here's another example:

Jessica's room <u>is</u> messy.

"Who or what is messy?" *Jessica's room.*

Which one word would you choose? Is *Jessica* messy? Maybe she is, but that's not what the sentence is about. Is the *room* messy? Yes.

Jessica's <u>room</u> <u>is</u> messy.

But if the subject is a person's name, underline the entire name:

> <u>Dr. Martin Luther King, Jr.</u>, <u>gave</u> his famous speech in 1963.

Now here is a tricky one:

> My favorite ride at Disney World <u>is</u> the Haunted Mansion.

"Who or what is the Haunted Mansion?" *Disney World* is the Haunted Mansion? No.

How about *my favorite ride* is the Haunted Mansion? Yes, but that's three words. Which one word would you choose? *Ride* is the best choice.

My favorite <u>ride</u> at Disney World <u>is</u> the Haunted Mansion.

Strange Subjects

Don't get confused if the subject is a word that looks like a verb. In grammar, we don't care what a word looks like. We only care about the job it is doing in the sentence. The job of a subject is to tell who or what performed the verb.

> Dancing <u>is</u> fun.

"Who or what is fun?" *Dancing* is fun. Underline the subject:

> <u>Dancing</u> <u>is</u> fun.

Try this sentence:

Cleaning the bathroom i̲s̲ disgusting.

"Who or what is disgusting?" *Cleaning the bathroom* is disgusting. Which one word would you choose? Is the *bathroom* disgusting? It might be, but this sentence is about *cleaning* the bathroom. Underline the subject:

C̲l̲e̲a̲n̲i̲n̲g̲ the bathroom i̲s̲ disgusting.

> **Getting tricky . . .**
>
> **Dancing** and **cleaning** are subjects, and they are also both nouns and **gerunds**. For an explanation of gerunds, see page 291.

Exercise 1.3 Finding Subjects

Double underline the verbs. Some sentences have one verb; others have two. Then, to find the subject, ask "Who or what performed the verb?" Some sentences have one subject; others have two or three. Underline just one word for each subject. Check your answers on page 315.

1. Professor Smith's literature class will study poetry.

2. The registrar spent two days fixing the schedules after the college's computer system crashed.

3. England established the first toll roads in 1269.

4. Dylan's favorite breakfast food is cold pizza.

5. Consumers in the United States discard nearly one hundred million cell phones annually.

6. Tiffany and Erika will work at Burger King this summer; Jasmine will serve as a camp counselor.

7. Sharing an apartment requires compromise.

8. Many people use the internet to reserve hotel rooms.

9. Germany and Japan recycle more than eighty percent of the glass and paper in their countries.

Exercise 1.4 Finding Subjects

Double underline the verbs. Some sentences have one verb; others have two. Then, to find the subject, ask, "Who or what performed the verb?" Some sentences have one subject; others have two or three. Underline just one word for each subject. Check your answers on page 316.

1. Jeremy bought a new phone last week.

2. His old phone dropped calls.

3. Melissa and Kari made an inexpensive desk out of a wooden door and two small file cabinets.

4. Friction between the brake pads and the wheel rims on a bicycle creates a bicycle's braking action.

5. On the day before Christmas, tape, scissors, and wrapping paper cluttered the dining room table.

6. Alonzo finished his calculus homework, and then he started his research paper on Napoleon.

7. In the 1960s Eartha Kitt and Cesar Romero made guest appearances on the *Batman* television series.

8. Chandra and Francis planned to go shopping, but their car's battery was dead.

9. After his computer crashed, Joseph tried writing his paper by hand.

10. When he got a cramp in his hand, Joseph went next door and borrowed his neighbor's laptop.

Chapter Two

✧

Phrases, Independent Clauses, and Dependent Clauses

I n this chapter you will learn two essential things:

1. the difference between a clause and a phrase

2. the difference between an independent clause and a dependent clause

Phrases, dependent clauses, and independent clauses are the building blocks that we use to make sentences. When you understand the difference between them, you will have the foundation for learning how to fix all kinds of sentence errors.

Clauses and Phrases

A **clause** is a group of words that has a subject and a verb.

A **phrase** is a group of words that doesn't have a subject and a verb.

We put clauses and phrases together to make sentences of different lengths. A very short sentence has just one clause. A very long sentence could have several clauses and several phrases.

To determine whether a group of words is a clause or a phrase, just look for a verb and a subject:

> The world's smallest dog is a Chihuahua.

Look for a verb by changing the time of the sentence:

> *Yesterday* The world's smallest dog **WAS** a Chihuahua.
>
> *Tomorrow* The world's smallest dog **WILL BE** a Chihuahua.

Double underline the word that changes:

> The world's smallest dog is a Chihuahua.

Now look for a subject. "Who or what is a Chihuahua?" *The world's smallest dog* is a Chihuahua. Which one word would you choose? *Dog.* Underline the subject:

> The world's smallest dog is a Chihuahua.

This group of words is a **clause** because it has a subject and a verb.

Now try this one:

> Lives in Kentucky

Look for a verb by changing the time:

> *Yesterday* **LIVED** in Kentucky
> *Tomorrow* **WILL LIVE** in Kentucky

Double underline the verb:

> <u>Lives</u> in Kentucky

Now look for a subject. "Who or what lives in Kentucky?" It doesn't say. This group of words doesn't have a subject, so it is not a clause; it's a **phrase**.

Here's one more example:

> Only four inches tall at the shoulders

Look for a verb by changing the time:

> *Yesterday* Only four inches tall at the shoulders
> *Every day* Only four inches tall at the shoulders
> *Tomorrow* Only four inches tall at the shoulders

Nothing changed. This group of words does not have a verb. It's a **phrase**. We don't need to bother looking for a subject. A clause needs a subject and a verb. If a group of words doesn't have a verb, it must be a phrase.

Exercise 2.1 Identifying Clauses and Phrases

Step 1) Change the time and listen for a verb. If you find a verb, <u>double</u> <u>underline</u> it.
If there is no verb, mark Ph for phrase, and you're finished with that one.

Step 2) If you have a verb, look for a subject by asking "who or what?" If you find a subject, <u>underline</u> it.
If there is no subject, mark Ph for phrase, and you're finished with that one.

Step 3) If you have a verb and a subject, mark C for clause.

Check your answers on page 317.

EXAMPLE: The smallest turtle in the U.S.   Ph

1. The bog turtle is the size of your palm   Ph – C

2. Lives in the soggy soil of wetlands   Ph – C

3. The Alabama beach mouse   Ph – C

4. Makes its home in grassy sand dunes   Ph – C

5. Construction threatens its habitat   Ph – C

6. Snow monkeys are native to Japan   Ph – C

7. Live farther north than any other monkey   Ph – C

8. Thick, soft fur for warmth   Ph – C

9. Snow monkeys bathe in the steaming water   Ph – C

10. Of Japan's natural hot springs   Ph – C

Prepositional Phrases

Any group of words that doesn't have a subject and a verb is a phrase. Traditional grammar has names for many different kinds of phrases, but for correct writing and punctuation, the kind of phrase doesn't matter.

However, it is useful to know **prepositional phrases.**

A **preposition** is a word that tells what a cat can do with a chair.

A cat can be
: **in** the chair
under the chair
beside the chair
near the chair
by the chair
with the chair

A cat can jump
: **over** the chair
on the chair
into the chair
off the chair
from the chair

A cat can run
: **around** the chair
to the chair
between two chairs

A cat can be so still that it looks like part
: **of** the chair

Other prepositions include **about, along, at, beyond, beneath, for, like, through,** and more.

A **prepositional phrase** is a group of words that starts with a preposition and then has a couple more words to complete the idea.

The subject or verb of a sentence will never be inside a prepositional phrase. So if you have a long sentence, you could first put parentheses around all the prepositional phrases. Then just look at the words left over to find the subject and verb.

> The <u>cat</u> <u>ran</u> (around the chair) and <u>jumped</u> (into my lap).
>
> The <u>mouse</u> <u>peeked</u> out (of his hole), <u>darted</u> (across the floor), and <u>disappeared</u> (under the couch.)
>
> The <u>man</u> <u>sat</u> (on the grass) (under a shady tree) (in Central Park) (on a beautiful day) (in mid-July) listening (to music).

Exercise 2.2 Identifying Prepositional Phrases

Put parentheses around the prepositional phrases, then mark the verbs and the subjects. Remember that neither the verb nor the subject will be inside a prepositional phrase. Check your answers on page 317.

1. Josie got lost in the old building.

2. The chess club will meet tomorrow in the library.

3. Max opened the heavy door, walked down the hall, went into the Registrar's office, sat in a chair, and waited his turn.

4. The mouse dashed out of the cat's paws and escaped into the woods.

5. Carrie placed her Hannah Montana CD collection in the trunk in the attic where she kept mementos from her childhood.

6. The archeologist found two vases of pure silver beneath a heap of rubble.

7. Renee took some yogurt out of the refrigerator, checked the expiration date, and dropped the yogurt into the trash can.

8. When the smoke detector in the chemistry lab rang, the students sitting near the alarm jumped in their seats.

9. The Lamborghini sped around the curves coming dangerously close to the edge of the cliff.

10. Rene Descartes, a mathematician with considerable talent, invented a branch of mathematics known as analytical geometry.

Getting tricky . . .

If you can't sleep nights because you have to know the names for all the different kinds of phrases in traditional grammar, turn to page 302.

Subordinating Conjunctions

Think of some words that begin with the prefix *sub.*

submarine   subway

These things go under. The submarine goes under the water; the subway goes under the street.

subservient   submissive

These words describe someone who is less powerful. A person who is subservient or submissive willingly obeys someone else.

The prefix *sub* means under, less powerful.

A **subordinating conjunction** is a word that goes at the beginning of a clause and makes the clause less powerful or dependent on another clause.

Common Subordinating Conjunctions

after	although	as	because
before	if	since	so that
that	though	till	until
unless	when	where	while

Independent and Dependent Clauses

As you know, a **clause** is any group of words that has a subject and a verb. There are two kinds of clauses—dependent and independent—and they have different sounds.

When you put a **subordinating conjunction** at the beginning of a clause, the clause will sound different.

> I ate dinner.
> After I ate dinner . . .

Say both of these clauses out loud and listen to how your voice sounds. When you say the first clause, the pitch of your voice goes down, and you sound like you're finished talking. The first clause expresses a complete idea.

When you say the second clause, the pitch of your voice goes up, and it sounds like you are going to continue speaking and tell what happened after you ate dinner. This clause does not express a complete idea. The listener is waiting for you to finish.

> After I ate dinner . . . what happened?

A **subordinating conjunction** is a word that goes at the beginning of a clause and makes the clause sound unfinished.

Mark subordinating conjunctions with a wavy underline.

A **dependent clause** is a clause that starts with a subordinating conjunction. It sounds unfinished and leaves the reader hanging. Mark dependent clauses **DC**.

An **independent clause** does not have a subordinating conjunction. It sounds complete. Mark independent clauses **IC**.

> After I ate dinner, I washed the dishes.
>   DC   IC

The first clause depends on the second clause to finish the idea.

Common Subordinating Conjunctions

after	although	as	because
before	if	since	so that
that	though	till	until
unless	when	where	while

Getting tricky . . .

See page 168 for information on False
Subordinating Conjunctions.

Exercise 2.3 Identifying Phrases, Independent Clauses, and Dependent Clauses

Step 1) Change the time and listen for a verb. If you find a verb, <u>double underline</u> it.
If there is no verb, mark **Ph** for phrase, and you're finished with that one.

Step 2) If you have a verb, look for a subject. Remember that the subject will almost always come before the verb. If you find a subject, <u>underline</u> it.
If there is no subject, mark **Ph** for phrase, and you're finished with that one.

Step 3) If you have a verb and a subject, it is a clause.
Now you must determine what kind of clause.
Look for a subordinating conjunction; it would be the
first word of the clause. If you find a subordinating
conjunction, underline it with a wavy line.

Step 4) If the clause has a subordinating conjunction, mark
DC for dependent clause. If there is no subordinating
conjunction, mark **IC** for independent clause.

Check your answers on page 318.

EXAMPLE: I hate mosquitos   **IC**

1. Always bite me   Ph – IC – DC

2. I try to kill them   Ph – IC – DC

3. When I am outside   Ph – IC – DC

4. Drive me crazy   Ph – IC – DC

5. While I mow the grass   Ph – IC – DC

6. I can't swat them   Ph – IC – DC

7. Because I have to push the mower   Ph – IC – DC

8. Before I go outside   Ph – IC – DC

9. I put on bug repellent spray   Ph – IC – DC

10. To keep the mosquitos away   Ph – IC – DC

Exercise 2.4 Identifying Phrases, Independent Clauses, and Dependent Clauses

Step 1) Change the time and listen for a verb.
If you find a verb, <u>double underline</u> it.
If there is no verb, mark **Ph** for phrase, and you're finished with that one.

Step 2) If you have a verb, look for a subject. Remember that the subject will almost always come before the verb.
If you find a subject, <u>underline</u> it.
If there is no subject, mark **Ph** for phrase, and you're finished with that one.

Step 3) If you have a verb and a subject, it is a clause.
Now you must determine what kind of clause.
Look for a subordinating conjunction; it would be the first word of the clause. If you find a subordinating conjunction, underline it with a wavy line.

Step 4) If the clause has a subordinating conjunction, mark **DC** for dependent clause. If there is no subordinating conjunction, mark **IC** for independent clause.

Check your answers on page 319.

EXAMPLE: The <u>Aztecs</u> <u>lived in</u> Mexico   **IC**

1. In the fifteenth and early sixteenth   Ph – IC – DC
    centuries

2. Since the Aztec society had a strict   Ph – IC – DC
    class structure

3. At the top level of society   Ph – IC – DC

4. The nobles were all related to the   Ph – IC – DC
    emperor

5. Although the nobles performed   Ph – IC – DC
    different jobs

6. Such as judge, priest, or soldier   Ph – IC – DC

7. Middle-class people were called   Ph – IC – DC
    commoners

8. Worked as farmers, merchants, and   Ph – IC – DC
    craftsmen

9. Slaves performed the hardest labor   Ph – IC – DC

10. Since they were at the bottom of the   Ph – IC – DC
    social structure

Exercise 2.5 Practice Identifying Phrases, Independent Clauses, and Dependent Clauses

Step 1) Change the tense and listen for a verb. If you find a verb, <u>double</u> <u>underline</u> it.
If there is no verb, mark **Ph** for phrase, and you're finished with that one.

Step 2) If you have a verb, look for a subject. Look for the subject in front of the verb. If you find a subject, <u>underline</u> it.
If there is no subject, mark **Ph** for phrase, and you're finished with that one.

Step 3) If you have a verb and a subject, it is a clause. Now you must determine what kind of clause.
Look for a subordinating conjunction; it would be the first word of the clause. If you find one, underline it with a <u>wavy line</u>.

Step 4) If the clause has a subordinating conjunction, mark **DC** for dependent clause. If there is no subordinating conjunction, mark **IC** for independent clause.

Check your answers on page 319.

EXAMPLE: Cell <u>phones</u> <u>are</u> everywhere   **IC**

1. The new phone was too complicated   Ph – IC – DC

2. For Johnna's mom to use   Ph – IC – DC

3. She gave the phone to Johnna   Ph – IC – DC

4. When the phone bill came   Ph – IC – DC

5. The bill was extremely high   Ph – IC – DC

6. Because Johnna sent too many texts   Ph – IC – DC

7. On the bus, during lunch, and even   Ph – IC – DC
   in class

8. To pay her mom back   Ph – IC – DC

9. Johnna found a job   Ph – IC – DC

10. At the cell phone kiosk in the mall Ph – IC – DC

The Sneaky, Mysterious, Invisible *That*

The word *that* can do many different jobs. It can be the subject of a sentence, or it can come at the end of a sentence.

> *That* is my car. I want to try *that*.

That can also be a subordinating conjunction. When *that* is functioning as a subordinating conjunction, is usually makes the second clause of a sentence dependent.

> I know that you ate my cookies!
> IC   DC

The word *that* has a tendency to go invisible.

> I know you ate my cookies!

We cannot see the word *that* in this sentence, but the meaning is still there. The second clause is still a dependent clause.

I <u>know</u> <u>you</u> <u>ate</u> my cookies!
  IC   DC

Pay attention when you speak and when you listen to others. You'll notice that people use the *invisible that* all the time.

Exercise 2.6 Identifying the Invisible *That*

<u>Double underline</u> the verbs and <u>underline</u> the subjects.

Write the word *that* under the sentence in the spot where it is invisible. One sentence has two dependent clauses and uses the invisible *that* two times. Check your answers on page 319.

EXAMPLE: <u>Gwendolyn</u> <u>knew</u> <u>Xavier</u> <u>loved</u> her.
                       that

1. For Valentine's day, Xavier knew Gwendolyn wanted roses.

2. But he was so broke he gave her freshly picked dandelions instead.

3. Gwendolyn was so disappointed she began to cry.

4. Xavier thought they were tears of joy she shed.

5. Gwendolyn wished Xavier was a little more romantic.

Chapter Three

✧

Fragments, Comma Splices, and Run-Ons

Fragments, comma splices, and run-ons are the most common mistakes that people make in their writing. In this chapter you will learn how to identify these mistakes and then how to fix them.

Sentence Fragments

A sentence must have an independent clause. A sentence that doesn't have an independent clause is called a **fragment**.

Remember:
An **independent clause** has a subject and a verb, and it expresses a complete idea.

> <u>Mario</u> <u>hit</u> the winning run.   IC
> The <u>weather</u> <u>was</u> cold.   IC

A **dependent clause** also has a subject and a verb, but it leaves the reader hanging. A dependent clause begins with a **subordinating conjunction** that changes the sound of the clause.

After Mario hit the winning run . . . what?   DC
Although the weather was cold . . . what?   DC

A **phrase** is any group of words that does not have a subject and a verb.

in the morning   Ph
wore a blue suit   Ph

Phrases and dependent clauses are important to our writing. They add details and make a sentence more interesting. But they cannot be sentences by themselves.

You will often see fragments in magazines, on billboards, and on your cereal box. If you are doing informal writing, go ahead and use fragments. For academic or business writing, it is better to write complete sentences.

Process for Identifying Fragments

Step 1)   Change the time and listen for a verb.
      If you find a verb, double underline it and go on to the next step.
      If there is no verb, the sentence is a phrase. Mark **F** for fragment.

Early in the morning.   **F**
After Mark <u>drove</u> all night.
(Go to the next step)

Step 2) Next, look for a subject by asking "who?" If you find a subject, <u>underline</u> it and go on to the next step. If there is no subject, the sentence is a phrase. Mark **F** for fragment.

Drove all night.   **F**
After <u>Mark</u> <u>drove</u> all night.
(Go to the next step.)

Step 3) If you have a verb and a subject, it is a clause. Now you must determine what kind of clause. Look for a subordinating conjunction. If you find one, underline it with a <u>wavy line</u>. If the clause has a subordinating conjunction, it is a dependent clause. Mark **F** for fragment.

<u>After</u> <u>Mark</u> <u>drove</u> all night.   **F**

Step 4) If the clause does not have a subordinating conjunction, it is an independent clause. Mark **OK** for a correct sentence.

<u>Mark</u> <u>drove</u> all night.   **OK**

Exercise 3.1 Identifying Fragments

Follow the steps: Double underline the verbs. Underline the subjects. Draw a wavy line under the subordinating conjunctions.

Mark phrases and dependent clauses **F**. Mark independent clauses **OK**. Check your answers on page 320.

EXAMPLE: The capybara is the world's largest rodent. **OK**

1. Weighs more than one hundred pounds. F – OK

2. Since its teeth grow continuously. F – OK

3. The capybara chews on tough grasses. F – OK

4. To keep its teeth short. F – OK

5. Capybaras live near rivers, lakes, and swamps. F – OK

6. In Central and South America. F – OK

7. They are excellent swimmers. F – OK

8. Because they have webbing between their toes. F – OK

9. When capybaras are alarmed. F – OK

10. They make a noise similar to a dog's bark. F – OK

Exercise 3.2 Identifying Fragments

Step 1) Change the time and listen for a verb. If you find a verb, <u>double underline</u> it. If there is no verb, the sentence is a phrase.

Mark **F** for fragment.

Step 2) If you have a verb, look for a subject. If you find a subject, <u>underline</u> it. If there is no subject, the sentence is a phrase.

Mark **F** for fragment.

Step 3) If you have a verb and a subject, it is a clause. Now you must determine what kind of clause. Look for a subordinating conjunction. If you find one, underline it with a <u>wavy line</u>.
If you have a subordinating conjunction, the clause is dependent.

Mark **F** for fragment.

Step 4) If there is no subordinating conjunction, the clause is independent.

Mark **OK** for correct sentence.

Check your answers on page 320.

EXAMPLE: Over 2,200 earthworm <u>species</u> <u>exist</u>.   **OK**

1. Earthworms live in all parts of the world.   F – OK

2. Except in the Arctic and extremely dry regions.   F – OK

3. Although worms in the tropics grow up to   F – OK
   ten or eleven feet long.

4. Most earthworms are shorter.   F – OK

5. Usually one to two inches in length.   F – OK

6. An earthworm is typically gray or reddish   F – OK
   brown in color.

7. Five tiny hearts pump the worm's blood.   F – OK

8. Because earthworms are responsible for   F – OK
   aerating and mixing the soil.

9. Earthworms are vital to agriculture.   F – OK

10. As Charles Darwin discovered when he   F – OK
    studied them.

Exercise 3.3 Identifying Fragments

Step 1) Double underline the verbs. If there is no verb, the
         sentence is a phrase.

         Mark **F** for fragment.

Step 2) Underline the subjects. If there is no subject, the sen-
         tence is a phrase.

         Mark **F** for fragment.

Step 3) Underline subordinating conjunctions with a wavy line.

         Mark the dependent clauses **F** for fragment.

Step 4) Mark the independent clauses **OK**.

Check your answers on page 320.

1. The British Invasion started in 1964.   F – OK

2. When the Beatles came to America.   F – OK

3. The Rolling Stones arrived next.   F – OK

4. Mick Jagger was the lead singer.   F – OK

5. In February of 1965.   F – OK

6. The Who led the second wave of the Invasion. F – OK

7. After they recorded the hit song "I Can't
    Explain."   F – OK

8. Next The Animals and The Hollies became   F – OK
    popular in the U.S.

9. American rocker Elvis Presley sold lots of   F – OK
    records in England.

10. Although he never performed there.   F – OK

Fixing Fragments

There are two ways to fix a fragment, and they both involve erasing something.

First Method: You can erase a period and attach the fragment to a sentence that has an independent clause.

> In the morning. <u>Sherry jogs</u> three miles.
> Ph-fragment   IC

Erase the period to attach the fragment to a complete sentence:

In the morning <u>Sherry</u> <u>jogs</u> three miles.
   Ph   IC

By joining the fragment to a complete sentence, you created one longer sentence. One independent clause is enough even for a very long sentence.

Here's another example:

<u>She</u> <u>goes</u> to the gym. <u>After</u> <u>she</u> <u>finishes</u> work.
  IC   DC-fragment

Erase the period to attach the fragment to the complete sentence:

<u>She</u> <u>goes</u> to the gym <u>after</u> <u>she</u> <u>finishes</u> work.
  IC   DC

By joining the fragment and a complete sentence, you created one longer sentence.

Second method: If the fragment is a dependent clause, you can erase the subordinating conjunction and turn the dependent clause into an independent clause.

<u>When</u> the <u>dog</u> <u>chews</u> the newspaper.
          DC-fragment

Erase the subordinating conjunction:

> The <u>dog</u> <u>chews</u> the newspaper.
> IC

Now the sentence has an independent clause, so it is correct.

Here's another example:

> After the <u>dog</u> <u>dug</u> up the flower bed.
> DC-fragment

Erase the subordinating conjunction:

> The <u>dog</u> <u>dug</u> up the flower bed.
> IC

Now the sentence has an independent clause, so it is correct.

Common Subordinating Conjunctions

after	**although**	**as**	**because**
before	**if**	**since**	**so that**
that	**though**	**till**	**until**
unless	**when**	**where**	**while**

Exercise 3.4 Fixing Fragments

Follow the steps: <u>Double underline</u> the verbs. <u>Underline</u> the subjects. Draw a <u>wavy line</u> under the subordinating conjunctions.

Any sentence that does not have an independent clause is a fragment. Fix the fragments by crossing out a period or by crossing out a subordinating conjunction.

Check your answers on page 321.

1. Alex, an African gray parrot, was thirty-one when he died. For thirty out of his thirty-one years. He lived in a research lab. At Brandeis University.

2. Scientist Irene Pepperberg taught him to speak. Pepperberg worked with Alex. To prove that animals had intelligence.

3. When Pepperberg showed him two objects. Like a green key and a green cup. Alex identified the similarity by saying "color." To show the difference between the two items. He spoke the word "shape."

4. Alex also counted and did simple arithmetic. When Alex died in 2007. He had learned to count to seven.

5. Alex's accomplishments seem incredible. Because a parrot's brain is the size of a walnut. Irene Pepperberg proved her point. That animals are capable of higher-level thinking.

Exercise 3.5 Fixing Fragments

Follow the steps: <u>Double underline</u> the verbs. <u>Underline</u> the subjects. Draw a <u>wavy line</u> under the subordinating conjunctions.

Any sentence that does not have an independent clause is a fragment. Fix the fragments by crossing out a period or by crossing out a subordinating conjunction.

Check your answers on page 321.

1. Gold has always fascinated humans. Because it is beautiful. Craftsmen in Mesopotamia used gold to create jewelry. As early as 3000 B.C.E.

2. Gold is valuable. Because it is rare. Throughout history, only about 160,000 tons of gold have been mined. Enough to fill two Olympic-sized swimming pools.

3. Isaac Newton first created a standard price for gold. Although most countries stopped tying their currency to the gold standard long ago. The United States maintained its gold standard until 1971.

4. Gold is usually found with other metals. Such as mercury or copper. Miners send the gold to smelters. For separating the gold from the other metals.

5. Although humans still want gold. Mining new gold has become more difficult. Costing more and causing more damage to the environment.

Comma Splices and Run-Ons

Unlike fragments, which don't have an independent clause, a **comma splice** and a **run-on** both have two independent clauses.

The only difference between a comma splice and a run-on is that a comma splice has a comma between the two independent clauses and a run-on does not have a comma.

Mark comma splices **CS** and run-ons **RO**.

> <u>Sue</u> <u>cooked</u> dinner, <u>Joe</u> <u>washed</u> the dishes.   **CS**
> IC   IC

> <u>Sue</u> <u>cooked</u> dinner <u>Joe</u> <u>washed</u> the dishes.   **RO**
> IC   IC

Getting tricky . . .

Some people use the term **fused sentence** or **run-together** for a run-on.

Four Methods for Fixing Comma Splices and Run-Ons

Comma splices and run-ons are easy to fix. Instead of erasing something as you did to fix fragments, you add something. There are four different things you can add to fix comma splices or run-ons.

First Method: Add a **period** at the spot where the two clauses meet to separate the two clauses into two sentences.

Sue <u>cooked</u> dinner, <u>Joe</u> <u>washed</u> the dishes.   **CS**
  IC   IC

Sue <u>cooked</u> dinner. <u>Joe</u> <u>washed</u> the dishes.   **OK**
  IC   IC

Second Method: Add a comma and a **coordinating conjunction** between the two independent clauses.

Coordinating Conjunctions

For   And   Nor   But   Or   Yet   So

The seven **coordinating conjunctions** are very special words. They are all short words—only two or three letters long. They are the ONLY words that can be used with a comma to separate two independent clauses.

You can use the acronym FANBOYS to remember them.

Sue <u>cooked</u> dinner, *and* <u>Joe</u> <u>washed</u> the dishes.   **OK**
  IC   IC

Sue <u>cooked</u> dinner, *so* <u>Joe</u> <u>washed</u> the dishes.   **OK**
  IC   IC

Coordinating conjunctions are the ONLY words that can be used with a comma to separate two independent clauses. A comma with any other word gives you a comma splice.

Sue <u>cooked</u> dinner, *therefore* <u>Joe</u> <u>washed</u> the dishes.   **CS**

Getting tricky . . .

SUB vs. CO

When we first learned about **subordinating conjunctions**, we looked at some words that begin with the prefix **sub**: submarine, subway, submissive.

We saw how the prefix **sub** means below or less powerful. A subordinating conjunction makes a clause less powerful—dependent—because the clause sounds unfinished.

After we watched the movie . . . . what happened?

Now think of some words that begin with the prefix **co**: cooperate, coworker, coexist.

The prefix **co** means together or equal. When you cooperate with someone, you work together. Your coworker is not your boss or your employee; you are equals. This is a very different meaning than sub.

A **coordinating conjunction** joins things that are equal, such as two independent clauses.

Third Method: You can add a **subordinating conjunction** at the beginning of one of the clauses to make the clause dependent. A comma splice or run-on occurs when you have two independent clauses. Make one of the clauses dependent, and you have solved the problem. Use whichever subordinating conjunction suits the meaning of your sentence.

<u>Sue</u> <u>cooked</u> dinner, <u>Joe</u> <u>washed</u> the dishes.   **CS**
IC   IC

<u>After</u> <u>Sue</u> <u>cooked</u> dinner, <u>Joe</u> <u>washed</u> the dishes.   **OK**
DC   IC

<u>Sue</u> <u>cooked</u> dinner <u>before</u> <u>Joe</u> <u>washed</u> the dishes.   **OK**
IC   DC

Notice the difference in the punctuation of these sentences. When the dependent clause comes first, we put a comma between the two clauses. When the independent clause comes first, we don't use a comma.

For more info on commas, turn to page 62.

Common Subordinating Conjunctions

after	**although**	**as**	**because**
before	**if**	**since**	**so that**
that	**though**	**till**	**until**
unless	**when**	**where**	**while**

Fourth Method: You can add a **semi-colon** (;) between the two clauses.

A semi-colon looks like exactly what it is. It is a half-way between a period and a comma. A semi-colon is big enough to separate the two independent clauses, but it is small enough that the two clauses are still one sentence.

Sue <u>cooked</u> dinner; Joe <u>washed</u> the dishes.   **OK**
　IC　　　　　　　　IC

For a variation on the semi-colon method, you can also add a **conjunctive adverb** and a comma. Use whichever word suits the meaning of the sentence.

Common Conjunctive Adverbs

however	therefore
consequently	furthermore
nevertheless	hence
accordingly	moreover

Sue <u>cooked</u> dinner; *therefore,* Joe <u>washed</u> the dishes.
　IC　　　　　　　　　　IC

Sue <u>cooked</u> dinner; *consequently,* Joe <u>washed</u> the dishes.
　IC　　　　　　　　　　　IC

Look carefully at the punctuation of these sentences. Put a semi-colon after the first independent clause. Then write the conjunctive adverb followed by a comma. Finally write the second independent clause.

Getting tricky . . .

The word **however** and the word **but** have essentially the same meaning. But when it comes to punctuation, they are totally different. **But** is a **coordinating conjunction**, one of those seven special little words that can be used with a comma to separate two independent clauses.

However is a **conjunctive adverb**. Conjunctive adverbs can't do anything in your sentence except sound impressive. Unlike coordinating conjunctions, they can't join independent clauses, and unlike subordinating conjunctions, they don't make a clause dependent. If you want to put a conjunctive adverb between two independent clauses, go ahead, but be sure that you use a semi-colon to separate the two clauses.

Process for Identifying Comma Splices and Run Ons

Step 1)   Change the time and listen for a verb.
Double underline the verbs.

After Jennifer <u>put</u> the clothes in the washer, she <u>pressed</u> the start button.

Step 2)   Next, look for a subject by asking "who?"
Underline the subjects.

> After <u>Jennifer</u> <u>put</u> the clothes in the washer, <u>she</u> <u>pressed</u> the start button.

Step 3)   Look at the beginning of each clause for a subordinating conjunction.
Mark any subordinating conjunction with a <u>wavy line</u>.

> <u>After</u> <u>Jennifer</u> <u>put</u> the clothes in the washer, <u>she</u> <u>pressed</u> the start button.

Step 4)   Count the Independent Clauses in the sentence.
If the sentence has only one independent clause, it is correct. Mark OK.
If it has two independent clauses, look at the spot where the two clauses come together.

Semi-colon	**OK**
Comma with FANBOYS	**OK**
Comma alone	**CS**
Nothing at all	**RO**

Exercise 3.6 Finding Comma Splices and Run-Ons

Follow the steps to analyze each sentence. <u>Double underline</u> the verbs and <u>underline</u> the subjects. Draw a <u>wavy line</u> under any subordinating conjunctions. Tell whether each sentence is OK, CS, or RO. Check your answers on page 322.

EXAMPLE: <u>Eyeglasses</u> <u>have</u> a long history Roman Emperor Nero <u>had</u> a pair in 60 C.E.   RO

1.   When Nero attended the gladiator games, the bright sun hurt his eyes.   OK CS RO

2.   He wore glasses with green lenses, the lenses blocked some of the light.   OK CS RO

3. The magnifying glass came much later; it was invented around 1000 C.E.   **OK CS RO**

4. Reading with a magnifying glass was inconvenient a monk got an idea around 1285.   **OK CS RO**

5. He used a piece of wire to hold two small magnifying lenses in front of his eyes.   **OK CS RO**

6. The monk invented the first pair of glasses, and his idea became popular very quickly.   **OK CS RO**

7. Since glasses were expensive, only rich people bought them.   **OK CS RO**

8. Eventually, the price came down more people wore glasses.   **OK CS RO**

9. Leonardo da Vinci imagined contact lenses in 1508, contacts were finally invented in 1895.   **OK CS RO**

10. Today optometry is an important medical field most Americans wear glasses or contacts.   **OK CS RO**

Exercise 3.7 Fixing Comma Splices and Run-Ons

Double underline the verbs and underline the subjects. Then fix each comma splice or run-on using one of the methods indicated.

A. semi-colon alone
   Dogs bark; cats meow.

B. semi-colon with a conjunctive adverb and comma
   Dogs bark; however, cats meow.

C. comma with a coordinating conjunction
Dogs bark, and cats meow.

D. period
Dogs bark. Cats meow.

E. subordinating conjunction on the first clause
Although dogs bark, cats meow.

F. subordinating conjunction on the second clause
Dogs bark while cats meow.

Check your answers on page 323.

EXAMPLE:

, but
Dinosaurs lived long ago they are extinct now.   (C)

1. Dinosaurs are classified as reptiles they were cold blooded.   (F or A)

2. Carnivorous dinosaurs typically had pointy teeth an herbivore's teeth were flat.   (E or C)

3. Dinosaurs laid eggs most mothers abandoned their nests.   (B or C)

4. Some dinosaurs have unusual features scientists are trying to figure out the purpose of those features.   (D or A)

5. Digging up dinosaur bones is only the beginning for paleontologists the real challenge is assembling the skeleton.   (A or F or D)

Exercise 3.8 Fixing Comma Splices and Run-Ons

<u>Double</u> <u>underline</u> the verbs and <u>underline</u> the subjects. Then fix each comma splice or run-on using one of the methods indicated.

A. semi-colon alone

B. semi-colon with a conjunctive adverb and comma

C. comma with a coordinating conjunction

D. period

E. subordinating conjunction on the first clause

F. subordinating conjunction on the second clause

Check your answers on page 323.

EXAMPLE:

<u>Benjamin Franklin</u> <u>was</u> a great man; <u>he</u> <u>lived</u> in Philadelphia. (A)

1. Franklin was born in 1706, he had sixteen brothers and sisters. (A or C)

2. Franklin wanted to be a writer he worked in his brother's printing shop. (C or E)

3. He was born in Boston Franklin moved to Philadelphia. (C or E)

4. In Philadelphia Franklin met and fell in love with Deborah, they got married. (B or D)

5. He started a newspaper it was called *The Pennsylvania Gazette*. (A or C)

6. The paper was successful, Franklin became famous. (E or B)

7. Franklin was also an inventor, he invented the wood stove. (A or C)

8. He discovered that lightning is electricity he invented the lightning rod. (B or C)

9. Franklin traveled to England, he advocated for better treatment of the American colonies. (A or F)

10. He signed the Declaration of Independence he also signed the U.S. Constitution. (A or D)

Exercise 3.9 Finding and Fixing Comma Splices and Run-Ons

This paragraph has a mixture of comma splices, run-ons, and correct sentences. Double underline the verbs, underline the subjects, and draw a wavy line under the subordinating conjunctions.

If a sentence has one independent clause, it is correct. Mark OK. If a sentence has two independent clauses, look carefully at how the two independent clauses are joined together.

Semi-colon	OK
Comma with FANBOYS	OK
Comma alone	CS
Nothing at all	RO

Fix the comma splices and run-ons any way you like. Check your answers on page 324.

Oreo cookies are delicious, people eat them in different ways. Some people eat the cookie in one bite, but other people nibble it slowly. Many children do the twist technique. They twist apart the two wafers they eat the cream filling first. When I was a kid, I ate the cream filling first. I left the chocolate wafers for my little brother, he was too young to know the difference. Today I like to dunk my Oreos in milk proper dunking requires skill. If you dunk for too long, the cookie falls apart in the glass of milk. Oreos were invented in 1912. For the first three years, consumers had a choice, they could get vanilla cream or lemon cream. Lemon cream was discontinued, so we had just the basic Oreo for many years. Then double stuff Oreos were invented they started an avalanche of new ideas for Oreos. Today consumers have many choices my favorite kind is still the original Oreos.

Common Subordinating Conjunctions

after	although	as	because
before	if	since	so that
that	though	till	until
unless	when	where	while

Coordinating Conjunctions

For   And   Nor   But   Or   Yet   So

Common Conjunctive Adverbs

however	therefore
consequently	furthermore
nevertheless	hence
accordingly	moreover

Chapter Four

✧

Commas

Commas can be tricky because we use them all the time to do many different jobs. One sentence may have three or more commas each doing a different job.

In this chapter you will first learn how to use basic commas—the four comma that we use most often. These commas are not too difficult, and they account for probably ninety percent of the commas you need for your writing.

The second part of the chapter covers advanced commas which are more complicated, but fortunately we don't need them as often.

At the end of the chapter, you will find instructions for using commas with dialogue and quotations.

Basic Commas

The first four comma jobs are the ones you will use most often in your writing, and they are easy to learn.

Comma Job #1

Commas separate **items in a list** of three or more things:

> I like candy, pie, and cake.

The items in the list might be one word each, or they might be more than one word:

> I like chocolate candy, apple pie, and carrot cake.

> I like eating chocolate candy, baking apple pies, and decorating cakes.

If you have more than three items in a list, put commas between all of them:

> I like candy, pie, cake, brownies, and ice cream.

If you have only two items in a list, don't put a comma:

> I hate spinach and liver.

Getting tricky . . .

Grammar books disagree about whether you should put a comma before the word **and** in a list. Some books say that the word **and** replaces the comma. Others say it is best to put the comma before the word **and**.

In this book you will see a comma before the word **and** in a list, but either style is correct.

If you're writing for school or business, ask your teacher or supervisor which style he or she prefers. For personal writing, use whichever style you prefer, but use it consistently.

Comma Job #2

Use a comma with a **coordinating conjunction** to join two independent clauses:

I <u>hate</u> cleaning the bathroom, *but* <u>I</u> <u>do</u> it every week.
  IC   IC

<u>Mike</u> <u>plays</u> first base, *and* <u>Devon</u> <u>plays</u> center field.
     IC   IC

Coordinating Conjunctions

For   And   Nor   But   Or   Yet   So

See page 49 for more information about coordinating conjunctions joining independent clauses.

Comma Job #3

Use a comma to separate the parts of **dates and place names**:

> Caroline was born on July 25, 1995.
> Caroline was born in Tacoma, Washington.

If the sentence continues after the year or the state, put another comma after the year or the state.

> Caroline was born on July 25, 1995, on a Tuesday.

> Caroline was born in Tacoma, Washington, at Tacoma General Hospital.

Comma Job #4

Use a comma after **introductory material** such as a phrase or a dependent clause that appears at the beginning of a sentence.

> Since he wants to stay fit, Mark exercises every day.
> DC   IC

> In order to stay fit, Mark exercises every day.
> Ph   IC

Always use a comma after an **introductory dependent clause**. With an **introductory phrase**, a comma is needed only if the phrase is more than four words long. For a shorter phrase, use a comma only if it is needed for clarity.

But always use a comma after the name of a person spoken to or after the word **yes, no**, or **well** at the beginning of a sentence:

> Floyd, please close your mouth when you chew.
> Well, why don't you take your elbows off the table?

Exercise 4.1 Basic Commas

Double underline the verbs, underline the subjects, and draw a wavy line under the subordinating conjunctions.

Think about what is going on in each sentence and which comma job applies. Add commas where they are needed and write the number of the comma job at the end of each sentence. If you don't know what job the comma is doing, don't put a comma in that sentence.

> Job #1 – list of three or more things
> Job #2 – independent clauses with a coordinating
>   conjunction
> Job #3 – dates and places
> Job #4 – introductory material

Some sentences will need several commas, and others won't need any.

Check your answers on page 325.

EXAMPLE:

On July 16, 2017, twelve <u>friends</u> <u>went</u> camping in the Northwest.
Job #3

1. First we unloaded all the gear from our cars and then we set up our tents.

2. Since we didn't have a shower we washed in the river.

3. For dinner we caught some catfish and fried them over the fire.

4. Fireflies crickets and frogs entertained us as we sat around a campfire.

5. We unpacked the marshmallows chocolate bars and graham crackers and made smores.

6. After our hands and mouths were thoroughly sticky people began to head toward their tents to sleep.

7. Everyone was sleeping soundly when rain began to fall.

8. One minute the rain fell in a drizzle and the next minute we were caught in a torrential downpour.

9. When the wind knocked over one tent everyone started to reconsider the wisdom of camping.

10. Around two in the morning we decided to pack up our tents and drive to Missoula Montana to stay in the Motel 6.

Exercise 4.2 Basic Commas

<u>Double underline</u> the verbs, <u>underline</u> the subjects, and draw a <u>wavy line</u> under the subordinating conjunctions.

Think about what is going on in each sentence and which comma job applies. Add commas where they are needed, and write the number of the comma job at the end of each sentence. If you don't know what job the comma is doing, don't put a comma in that sentence.

> Job #1 – list of three or more things
> Job #2 – independent clauses with a coordinating
> conjunction
> Job #3 – dates and places
> Job #4 – introductory material

Some sentences will need several commas, and others won't need any.

Check your answers on page 326.

EXAMPLE:

<u>Gerbils</u> <u>are</u> hard to catch <u>because</u> <u>they</u> <u>are</u> little, fast, and slippery.   *Job #1*

1. On May 15 2017 we came home from the grocery store to find that our pet gerbil had escaped from his cage.

2. Leo had chewed a hole in his cage so we closed the front door to keep him from running outside.

3. Since we couldn't open the door we passed the grocery bags in through an open window.

4. As soon as we put the groceries away we started looking for Leo.

5. We looked under the couch behind the dresser and in the bathtub.

6. We even looked under all the dirty clothes on my brother's bedroom floor.

7. We didn't find Leo but we found three dimes a marble and a stale granola bar.

8. After several hours of searching we gave up.

9. Before going to sleep we rigged up a gerbil trap and filled it with sunflower seeds.

10. We woke up on May 16 2017 to find Leo sleeping in the trap and we bought him a stronger cage that same day.

Advanced Commas

Next we will learn three advanced comma jobs. These are somewhat tricky, but you won't need them too often in your writing.

Comma Job #5

Use one or two commas to separate a **conjunctive adverb** from the sentence. Conjunctive adverbs are impressive-sounding words that show the relationship between ideas.

Common Conjunctive Adverbs

however	therefore
consequently	furthermore
nevertheless	hence
accordingly	moreover

First we will look at conjunctive adverbs in a sentence with just one clause.

If the conjunctive adverb comes at the beginning or end of the sentence, separate it with one comma. If the conjunctive adverb comes in the middle of the clause, separate it with a comma before and a comma after.

Consequently, Miss America will relinquish her crown effective immediately.

The Miss America crown, *therefore*, will go to the first runner up.

The former Miss America will keep her bouquet of roses, *however*.

Conjunctive adverbs can also be used between two independent clauses. In this case, use a semi-colon before the conjunctive adverb and a comma after.

The temperature was 105 degrees; *consequently*, we postponed the hike.

I want to go to the party; *however*, I have to finish my homework first.

If you're having a déjà vu experience, it's because you already learned this on page 52.

Comma Job #6

Use a comma to separate **coordinate adjectives**.

An **adjective** is a word that modifies or describes a noun. **Coordinate** means equal. Adjectives are common, but it is rare for them to be coordinate.

The dog had tangled dirty fur.

In this sentence *tangled* and *dirty* are both adjectives describing the fur.

There are two tests you can use to determine if the adjectives are coordinate. The first test is to reverse the words:

The dog had dirty tangled fur.

That sounds okay. The second test is to say the word *and* between the two adjectives:

The dog had tangled and dirty fur.

That sounds okay. These two adjectives passed the tests. They are coordinate, so you should put a comma between them:

The dog had tangled, dirty fur.

Here is another sentence.

> He wore a new blue suit.

Use the two tests to see if the adjectives *new* and *blue* are equal. First, reverse the words:

> He wore a blue new suit.

That sounds funny. Try the second test:

> He wore a new and blue suit.

That sounds funny too. These adjectives did not pass the tests. They are not coordinate, so don't put a comma between them:

> He wore a new blue suit.

What if the two adjectives pass one test but not the other? That hardly ever happens, but if it does, you can decide whether to put the comma or not. In the vast majority of cases, two adjectives will not be coordinate.

For more info on adjectives, see page 309.

Comma Job #7

Use commas to separate **non-essential material** from the sentence. **Non-essential** means extra, not necessary to the meaning of the sentence.

Kids *who watch TV all day* are lazy.

To determine whether you should put commas around the middle part of this sentence, you must decide if those words are extra. Would the meaning of the sentence change if you removed those middle words?

Kids are lazy.

This sentence does not have the same meaning as the original sentence. It sounds as if all kids are lazy, not just kids who watch TV all day. Since these words are not extra, you should not put commas around them:

Kids who watch TV all day are lazy.

Here is another one.

Jason *who watches TV all day* is lazy.

Here you see the same words in the middle of the sentence. What happens if you take them out this time?

Jason is lazy.

This sentence doesn't tell us why Jason is lazy, but the meaning is the same. In this case, those middle words are extra, or non-essential, so you should put commas around them:

Jason, who watches TV all day, is lazy.

One particular type of non-essential element is an **appositive**, a word or group of words that renames somebody or something. Sometimes an appositive is extra (non-essential) and sometimes it is needed.

My brother Louis teaches SCUBA diving.

The appositive here is *Louis*. I already named him once when I said *my brother*. When I give his first name, I am naming him again. That's an appositive.

Now I have to decide if *Louis* is extra or not. The real question is how many brothers do I have? If I have two brothers, the reader wouldn't know which brother I mean. His name would not be extra, so I would not put commas.

Here's my sentence if I have two brothers:

My brother Louis teaches SCUBA diving.

But if I have only one brother, there is only one person I could mean by *my brother*. In this case, the name *Louis* would be extra, so I would put commas around his name.

Here's my sentence if I have only one brother:

My brother, Louis, teaches SCUBA diving.

Your use of commas tells the reader whether you have one brother or more than one.

Be careful—When you're looking for non-essential elements, don't get carried away. Look at this sentence:

Jennifer has a red car.

What word in the middle of this sentence could be left out? *Red*. But should you put commas around the word *red*? No.

Commas have a certain sound to them. They tell the reader to put a little pause or give a little emphasis. If you pause before and after the word *red*, the sentence will sound strange:

Jennifer has a . . . *RED* . . . car.

When you're considering putting commas around something in the middle of a sentence, first make sure it really is extra, and then also think about whether you want the sound of commas there.

Common Conjunctive Adverbs

however	therefore
consequently	furthermore
nevertheless	hence
accordingly	moreover

Exercise 4.3 Advanced Commas

Think about what is going on in each sentence and which comma job applies. Add commas where they are needed, and write the number of the comma job at the end of each sentence.

> Job #5 – conjunctive adverbs
> Job #6 – coordinate adjectives
> Job #7 – non-essential material

Some sentences will need one comma, some will need two, and others won't need any.

Check your answers on page 326.

EXAMPLE: Monica brushed her long, shiny hair.   *Job #6*

1. The noisy excited kids crowded into the movie theater.

2. That old blue car is good enough for driving to work.

3. My mother the lady in the pink suit is the keynote speaker.

4. People who live in glass houses shouldn't throw stones.

5. Football players therefore spend a great deal of time in the weight room.

6. Dogs that bark all night long drive me crazy.

7. Domesticated dogs which are descended from wolves are good family pets.

8. The landlord finally replaced the apartment's orange shag carpet.

9. The imitation paneling however will not be replaced until next year.

10. People who don't brush and floss have a much higher incidence of cavities.

This exercise was challenging. Commas can be tricky, so don't be discouraged if you had problems. Check your answers and try to understand any mistakes you made.

Exercise 4.4 Advanced Commas

Think about what is going on in each sentence and which comma job applies. Add commas where they are needed, and write the number of the comma job at the end of each sentence.

> Job #5 – conjunctive adverbs
> Job #6 – coordinate adjectives
> Job #7 – non-essential material

Some sentences will need one comma, some will need two or three, and others won't need any.

Check your answers on page 327.

EXAMPLE: Monica brushed her long, shiny hair.   *Job #6*

1. The patient walked into the cold cramped waiting room.

2. Abraham Lincoln author of the Gettysburg Address is considered one of America's greatest orators.

3. San Francisco however has a much cooler climate than Los Angeles.

4. The barista squirted heavy whipping cream onto the steaming vanilla latte.

5. Mary wore a long black gown to the long boring opera.

6. The granite countertops a last minute addition sent the new house over budget.

7. Roberto scanned the bleachers of the school's gym for his girlfriend Jasmine and her friends.

8. Consequently the teacher suggested that Monica get an early start on writing her long complicated research paper.

9. The girl who brought a snake to school received two days of suspension.

10. The soft lights in the counselor's office however contrasted with her loud bossy personality.

Common Conjunctive Adverbs

however	therefore
consequently	furthermore
nevertheless	hence
accordingly	moreover

Commas in Dialogue and Quotations

Dialogue means a conversation between people. If you write a short story or a novel, you will probably want to include conversations between your characters.

When you write a research paper, you may want to include **quotations**, words that a knowledgeable or important person wrote or spoke about your topic.

Comma usage is the same for both dialogue and quotations. Look at these examples:

"Let's go out to eat. I don't feel like cooking," said Becca.

"Do you want to get pizza or Chinese food?" asked Mark.

Becca answered, "Pizza sounds good."

"Give me liberty, or give me death," said Patrick Henry.

"Give me liberty, or give me death!" said Patrick Henry.

Patrick Henry said, "Give me liberty, or give me death!"

Use a comma to separate the **signal phrase** (who said it) from the words spoken. If the signal phrase comes after the words spoken, put the comma inside the quotation marks. But if you already have a question mark or an exclamation point in that spot, you don't need to add a comma.

For more information on punctuating dialogue, see page 95.

Why Commas Drive People Crazy

Each comma job by itself is not too difficult. But it is quite common for a sentence to need several commas, each one doing a different job. The challenging aspect of commas is figuring out what's going on in your sentence and which comma job applies.

Exercise 4.5 Analyzing Comma Jobs

In the sentences below, the commas are already in their correct places. Figure out which job each comma is doing and write the number of that job at the end of the sentence.

> Job #1 – list of three or more things
> Job #2 – two independent clauses with a coordinating
> conjunction
> Job #3 – dates and places
> Job #4 – introductory material
> Job #5 – conjunctive adverb
> Job #6 – coordinate adjective
> Job #7 – non-essential material

Check your answers on page 328.

EXAMPLE: While Felix washed the cars, Pam cleaned the kitchen, living room, and bathrooms.   *Job #4 & #1*

1. Benjamin Franklin was born in Boston, Massachusetts, but he later moved to Philadelphia, Pennsylvania.

2. Monkeys have tails, but gorillas do not have tails; they are both primates, however.

3. People who can't drive must take the bus, the train, or the subway.

4. While Gloria looked in the mirror, the hairdresser styled her long, beautiful hair.

5. Melissa's husband, Todd, likes to fish, hunt, and hike.

6. After hiking all day, Todd soaked his swollen, aching feet.

7. They met February 14, 2014, at a party, and they were married on February 14, 2015.

8. I had not planned to go out this evening; I could, however, be persuaded.

9. On the first day of kindergarten, Maria watched her eldest daughter, Katie, get on the school bus.

10. Daniel washed the car, mowed the grass, and trimmed the bushes; consequently, his muscles were sore that evening.

Chapter Five

✧

Other Punctuation and Mechanics

This chapter covers all the other punctuation marks besides commas—apostrophes, dashes, colons, and semi-colons—as well as the rules for capitalization, punctuating dialogue, and writing out numbers.

Apostrophes

We use apostrophes in contractions and to show possession.

Apostrophe Job #1

Use an apostrophe to indicate where letters have been removed to form a contraction.

I do not play chess.   I don't play chess.

Most contractions are easy, but some are tricky:

I would   **I'd**
I'd love to go to Hawaii for vacation.

I had   **I'd**
I'd already paid for my groceries when I remembered my coupons.

He would   **he'd**
He'd rather play golf than mow the lawn.

She had   **she'd**
She'd already lost four golf balls before she reached the second hole.

Let us   **let's**
Let's go out for dinner tonight.

You are   **you're**
You're not wearing that to the party, are you?
Use an apostrophe when you mean YOU ARE.

It is   **it's**
It's so hot today; let's go swimming.
Use an apostrophe when you mean IT IS.

They are   **they're**
They're saving up to buy a house.
Use an apostrophe when you mean THEY ARE.

When we're talking, we use contractions all the time. In writing, it is not wrong to use contractions, but they do make your writing sound rather informal. In a paper for school or a business letter, it's usually best to avoid contractions.

> **Getting tricky . . .**
>
> **You're, it's,** and **they're** are tricky because they have homophones: words that sound the same but have different spellings and different meanings. The chapter on homophones begins on page 149.

Apostrophe Job #2

Use **'s** to indicate possession.

Possession includes not only ownership of a material object but also relationships and ideas:

> **Material Possessions:**
> Billy's tricycle
> Carrie's house
> the library's books
> the dog's bone
>
> **Relationships:**
> Ethan's mom
> Linda's sister
> the car's driver
> the company's staff

Ideas and Non-Material Things:
Selma's responsibility
Bob's problem
Grace's concern
the cat's personality
the nation's economic outlook

When you start thinking about apostrophes, it is tempting to put an apostrophe in every word that ends with an **s**. If the **s** is just indicating plural, not possession, don't put an apostrophe.

> That is Adam's bike.
>> Does Adam own anything?
>> Yes. Adam owns a bike; use an apostrophe.

> Two cars were in the garage.
>> Do the cars own anything?
>> No, there is just more than one of them.
>> Don't use an apostrophe.

> Three mayors had a conference.
>> Do the mayors own anything?
>> No, there is just more than one of them.
>> Don't use an apostrophe.

> The cat's food bowl is empty.
>> Does the cat own anything?
>> Yes. The cat owns a bowl.
>> Use an apostrophe.

Possession with Words Ending in S

If a word ends with the letter **s**, you don't need to add another **s**. Just put an apostrophe at the end of the word to indicate possession.

Carlos owns a dog.	Carlos' dog
Dennis owns a stereo.	Dennis' stereo
Mr. Jones owns a car.	Mr. Jones' car

Sometimes the word ends with **s** because two people own something together. Imagine two dogs who share their dog house.

Two dogs own a house.	Dogs' house

Just as with the name *Carlos*, the word *dogs* ends with an **s**. You don't need to add another **s**; just add the apostrophe. But be careful to place the apostrophe at the end of the word: dogs'.

Actually, the placement of the apostrophe shows whether one or two or more dogs (or people) own something because the apostrophe marks the end of the word. Does the dog have his own house, or does he have to share?

My cat's ball	Look at the letters that come before the apostrophe: cat. That's one cat. She has her own ball.
The boys' bedroom	Look at the letters that come before the apostrophe: boys. That's more than one boy. Two (or more) boys are sharing.

Exercise 5.1 Apostrophes

Add apostrophes where they are needed. Some sentences need more than one apostrophe, and others don't need any. Check your answers on page 329.

1. The announcers voice echoed throughout the stadium.

2. The Beatles first appeared on Ed Sullivans variety show on August 24, 1964.

3. Jack Parr—Ed Sullivans main rival—had aired footage of the Beatles in January 1964.

4. The professors car was towed because it was parked in the students lot.

5. Sams cats favorite game is clawing the drapes.

6. The name Matthew means "Gods gift," while Samanthas meaning is "God heard us."

7. England has had six kings named George.

8. "Lets review for the test," announced the professors assistant.

9. Graphing calculators are essential for students in upper-level math classes.

10. Even though Frances owned a car, she had to borrow her roommates car for trips over five miles.

Exercise 5.2 Apostrophes

Add apostrophes where they are needed. Some sentences need more than one apostrophe, and others don't need any. Check your answers on page 330.

1. The authors previous lectures had been wildly successful.

2. Six hundred people purchased their tickets months in advance to reserve their spots.

3. Early in the morning, the auditoriums air conditioning units malfunctioned.

4. The programs producer called a repair crew.

5. When the repair techs arrived, they couldnt fix the air conditioners because they didnt have the right parts.

6. Sweat dripped down the authors face as she began the lecture.

7. Some paramedics arrived to treat a man who had fainted in the auditoriums stifling heat.

8. The author didnt want any lawsuits, so she stopped in the middle of the speech and asked the box office to refund the audiences money.

9. The peoples impatience with the two employees trying to issue refunds created an even more unpleasant situation.

10. When they left, everyone had experienced the authors message: global warming.

Exercise 5.3 Plural Possessives

In the following sentences, look at the letters that come before the apostrophe. Then mark **one** or **more than one**.

Check your answers on page 331.

EXAMPLE:

The **dog**'s bowl is blue.   **one dog**
                                               more than one

1. The cats' clawing pole is ragged.   one cat
                                               more than one

2. The goose's honk was loud.   one goose
                                               more than one

3. The student's work was correct.   one student
                                               more than one

4. The women's restroom was crowded.   one woman
                                               more than one

5. The birds' nest was on a branch.   one bird
                                               more than one

6. The squirrel's nest was in a tree.   one squirrel
                                               more than one

7. The children's playroom was messy.   one child
                                          more than one

8. The man's coat was warm.   one man
                                          more than one

Capitalization

Capitalization is one of the first things children learn in school. Most of the capitalization rules are very easy, but a few of them can cause problems for writers.

Capitalization Rule #1

Use a capital letter for people's names and titles that precede the name:

Mr. Smith	Rev. Jones
Miss Baxter	King Henry
Senator Brown	President Washington
Uncle Charley	Principal Jackson

Capitalization Rule #2

Use a capital letter for family titles when you could replace the title with the person's first name.

When Mom and Dad got home, Grandma said the kids had been very good.

In this sentence, the family titles are capitalized because it sounds fine to replace the family titles with the first names:

When Mary and Steve got home, Barbara said the kids had been very good.

Here is another sentence:

My Mary gave my Steve a sweater for his birthday.

This sounds funny. Don't capitalize the family titles in this sentence because you can't replace them with the names.

My mom gave my dad a sweater for his birthday.

Capitalization Rule #3

Use a capital letter for the days of the week, the months of the year, and for holidays:

Monday   April   Independence Day

Capitalization Rule #4

Capitalize the names of ethnic groups, nationalities, and languages:

African-American   Chinese
Spanish   Asian
British   Arabic
Latino   Polynesian
English   Caucasian
Australian   Greek

What about the words *black* and *white* when referring to race? Whether you capitalize these words depends on whom you're writing for. When writing for school, don't capitalize them unless your teacher tells you to. If you are writing for a publication that capitalizes these words as part of its official style, then follow that style.

Capitalization Rule #5

Capitalize the names of specific things, but don't capitalize general things.

Specific Things:	General Things:
Africa	continent
Pacific Ocean	ocean
Spain	country
Mount Kilimanjaro	mountain
Paris	city
Main Street	street
the Empire State Building	office building
S.S. Titanic	ship
Starship Enterprise	spaceship
Magic Shears Hair Salon	beauty parlor
Nikes	tennis shoes
Wheaties	cereal
President Washington	the president
Christianity	religion
Jewish	faith
Episcopal	church

Capitalization Rule #6

Capitalize the first word and the important words in the title of a book, movie, etc.

> *Of Mice and Men*
> *Better Homes and Gardens*
> *Raiders of the Lost Ark*

Did you know?

Italicize (or underline) the title of a long work, such as a book, magazine, movie, or CD:

The Grapes of Wrath (book)
Sports Illustrated (magazine)
Titanic (movie)
Blues Train (CD)

Put quote marks around the titles of short works or works that appear inside a larger work such as an article in a magazine or newspaper, a song on a CD, etc.:

"Carter wins Nobel Prize" (magazine article)
"Fast Train" (song on a CD)

Exercise 5.4 Capitalization

Capitalize words as needed. Check your answers on page 331.

1. for christmas aunt josephine gave my mother a poodle named ruffles.

2. many american companies have factories in other countries; for example, some texas instruments calculators are made in utrecht, netherlands.

3. next monday school will end at 11:30 so that the teachers can meet with parents while superintendent toni godwin meets with the administrators.

4. vincent d'onofrio plays robert goren, one of TV's most fascinating detectives; his partner, alex eames, played by kathryn erbe, has been called the dr. watson to goren's sherlock holmes.

5. Many english words have spanish origins, including alligator, plaza, and stampede.

Exercise 5.5 Capitalization

Capitalize words as needed. Check your answers on page 332.

EXAMPLE: This year Christmas is on a Monday.

1. we will go to grandma's house for dinner.

2. my grandma makes great christmas cookies.

3. for thanksgiving mom always bakes pumpkin pie.

4. my dad loves thanksgiving because he likes to eat.

5. miss dixon went to tokyo on her vacation.

6. most of the people in israel are jewish.

7. on wednesdays i go to my spanish class.

8. columbus sailed to america with the nina, the pinta, and the santa maria.

9. many asian people live in san francisco.

10. we could go to an italian restaurant, a mexican restaurant, or a french restaurant.

Punctuating Dialogue

Dialogue is words spoken out loud. Follow these guidelines for puntuating dialogue:

1. Start a new paragraph each time a different person speaks.

2. Put quotation marks around the words spoken.

3. Begin the spoken words with a capital letter.

4. Place a period, question mark, exclamation point, comma, or semi-colon inside the quotation marks.

5. Separate the *he said/she said* from the words spoken with a comma (or question mark, etc.).

6. You can omit the *he said/she said* as long as the reader will be able to tell who is saying what.

The easiest way to learn how to punctuate dialogue is to follow the example of any novel.

> Maggie and Jackie were standing at the corner waiting for the bus. It was a cold November morning, and the wind was howling.
> "My fingers are freezing!" Maggie said.
> Jackie agreed, "Mine too, and my nose is like ice."
> "It seems like we've been waiting for twenty minutes," Maggie said.
> "I know. I wonder if the bus is late or if it's just because we're so cold," said Jackie.

"Do you have a watch on?" Maggie asked.

"No," answered Jackie, "but I'll look on my cell phone."

"Wait!" Maggie said, "here it comes now." They watched as the bus came around the corner.

"It's coming awfully fast," said Jackie. The bus hit a patch of ice and spun in a circle before coming to a stop.

For information about punctuating quotations in a research paper, see pages 204–206. For information about using commas in dialogue and quotations, turn to page 78.

Numbers

Spell numbers that can be expressed with one or two words:

| one | thirty-three | two thousand |
| seventeen | one hundred | five million |

If three or more words are needed to express a number, use numerals instead.

| 101 | 3, 015 | 7,429 | 5,000,003 |

But always spell out a number that is the first word of the sentence.

Nineteen sixty-four was a great year.
I was born in **1964**.

Hyphens and Dashes

A **hyphen** is used to join words:

sister-in-law	five-year-old
two-fifths	pre-2001
un-American	president-elect

A **dash** is used to separate parts of a sentence. Make a dash by typing two hyphens. Many computer programs will join the two hyphens together into one long dash.

A dash can be used in the same places you would use a comma, but a dash gives a longer pause and a greater sense of emphasis. Use a dash when you want a dramatic effect:

> I have had quite an exciting day—but you wouldn't want to hear about it, would you?

> Marcus said—brace yourself!—he has been accepted to Harvard!

> Her three best friends—Jill, Jan, and Joan—gave her a surprise birthday party.

Colons

Colons are more formal than dashes. A colon is used only after an independent clause; the first part of the sentence must be able to stand alone. The colon introduces a list or an example.

> Her essay contained numerous grammatical errors: comma splices, fragments, and misspellings, just to name a few.

> I have three favorite authors: Dickens, Steinbeck, and Austen.

> There was only one hope: we had to find an antidote.

Notice that in each of these sentences, the first part could stand alone. It is an independent clause with a complete idea:

> Her essay contained numerous grammatical errors.
> I have three favorite authors.
> There was only one hope.

For an explanation of independent clauses, turn to page 28.

Here are some sentences in which a colon is used incorrectly. See if you can tell what's wrong:

> Her essay contained numerous grammatical errors such as: comma splices, fragments, and misspellings.

> My three favorite authors are: Dickens, Steinbeck, and Austen.

> Our only hope was: we had to find an antidote.

Do you see what's wrong? The words before the colon do not express a complete idea by themselves:

> Her essay contained numerous grammatical errors such as.
>
> My three favorite authors are.
>
> Our only hope was.

In these sentences the words before the colon can not stand alone, so a colon is not appropriate. Actually, no punctuation is needed:

> Her essay contained numerous grammatical errors such as comma splices, fragments, and misspellings.
>
> My three favorite authors are Dickens, Steinbeck, and Austen.
>
> Our only hope was we had to find an antidote.

One other use for a colon is to set off the subtitle of a book. Many non-fiction books will have a title and a subtitle. The cover of the book looks like this:

A World Lit Only by Fire

The Medieval Mind and the Renaissance
by William Manchester

If you need to give the name of this book in a sentence, punctuate it like this:

I just finished reading *A World Lit Only by Fire: The Medieval Mind and the Renaissance* by William Manchester.

Even though the title is not italicized on the cover of the book, you should italicize (or underline) the title in your writing. For info on italicizing or using quote marks around titles, see page 92.

Semi-Colons

A period and a comma met at a party. They fell in love, got married, and had a beautiful baby that was a semi-colon. A semi-colon is halfway between a period and a comma. It is smaller than a period but bigger than a comma.

Semi-Colon Job #1

The most common use of a semi-colon is to separate two independent clauses as explained on page 52.

<u>Jill</u> <u>wanted</u> Mexican food; <u>Jason</u> <u>wanted</u> pizza.
   IC   IC

Semi-Colon Job #2

Semi-colons are also used to separate items in a list when the items contain commas, such as place names:

I've lived in Tallahassee, Florida; Tacoma, Washington; and Raleigh, North Carolina.

Normally items in a list would be separated by commas as explained on page 62. But in this case, using only commas would make the sentence confusing:

> I've lived in Tallahassee, Florida, Tacoma, Washington, and Raleigh, North Carolina.

This sentence reads like six places rather than three places with two names each. Semi-colons divide up the list more clearly.

Exercise 5.6 Colons, Dashes, and Semi-Colons

Add colons, dashes, and semi-colons where needed. Some sentences need more than one type of punctuation mark. One sentence does not need any additional punctuation.

Check your answers on page 332.

1. The most popular sports in America are football, basketball, and baseball.

2. America's most popular sports football, basketball, and baseball are viewed by millions every year.

3. As an executive assistant for marketing, Jaime has traveled to three major international cities this year Lima, Peru Sydney, Australia and Rome, Italy.

4. Hillside High's Brad Pitt no relation to the famous actor has three favorite teachers Mr. Smith, Mrs. Wilkins, and Ms. Cassidy.

5. The week before Christmas, the malls are packed with people buying gifts the week after Christmas, the malls are packed with people returning gifts.

6. My old car got twelve miles per gallon my new car gets thirty.

7. Stefan a true coffee snob will only drink Starbuck's espresso.

8. Only one thing kept me from flying to Acapulco for spring break I didn't have any money.

9. Jan spent her spring break in Acapulco she went to Aspen for Christmas.

10. When you're buying real estate, only three things matter location, location, and location.

Chapter Six

✧

Case, Agreement, and Irregular Verbs

This chapter covers pronoun case, pronoun–antecedent agreement, and subject–verb agreement.

Pronouns

A **pronoun** is a word that replaces another word:

> Superman is faster than a speeding bullet.
> He is more powerful than a locomotive.
> He can leap tall buildings in a single bound.

He is the pronoun that replaces the word *Superman*.

Superman is the **antecedent** (ant-eh-SEE-dent). The prefix *ante* means before, so the antecedent is the word that comes before the pronoun. The antecedent is the word that the pronoun is replacing.

When you're writing, make sure that your reader can easily identify the antecedent for each pronoun.

> Sue, Sally, and Samantha went rollerblading.
> She fell and broke her wrist.

In the second sentence, the pronoun is *she*, but the antecedent is unclear. You can't tell which woman fell. This mistake is called **unclear pronoun reference** because it is unclear which antecedent the pronoun is referring to. In this type of sentence, use the person's name instead of a pronoun.

> Sue, Sally, and Samantha went rollerblading.
> Sally fell and broke her wrist.

For more information on pronouns and the nouns they replace, see page 305.

Did you know?

We use the prefix **ante** all the time: I woke up at 7 a.m.

The abbreviation a.m. stands for ante meridian. **Ante** means before, and **meridian** means middle of the day or noon.

The abbreviation p.m. stands for post meridian. **Post** means after.

Pronoun Case

Pronouns can be tricky because different forms of the pronoun need to be used for different functions in a sentence. This is called **pronoun case.**

If the pronoun is serving as the subject of the sentence, we use **subjective case**:

> *I* took my dog with me.

If the pronoun is showing ownership, we use **possessive case**:

> I took *my* dog with me.

If the pronoun comes at the end of a clause or phrase, we typically use **objective case**:

> I took my dog with *me.*

These three pronouns—*I, my, me*—all refer to the same person, but we need all three words because each pronoun is serving a different function. If you mix up the cases, the sentence will sound funny:

> Me took I dog with my.

If English is your first language, you automatically use the correct case for pronouns most of the time:

You took your dog with you.
He took his dog with him.
She took her dog with her.
We took our dog with us.
They took their dog with them.

You don't often hear people say:

Me washed the car.
Him washed the car.
You can ride to the game with I.
You can ride to the game with he.

But when a sentence has two names together, choosing the correct case is not so easy. You may often hear people make mistakes:

Me and Mike washed the car.
Mike and him washed the car.

You can ride to the game with Joe and I.
You can ride to the game with he and Joe.

Choosing the Correct Case

To choose the correct pronoun case in a sentence that has another name, leave out that other name, and you will know which pronoun sounds right:

Sheila went shopping with Rachel and (I or me?)

Leave out Rachel's name to see what sounds right.

> Sheila went shopping with I.

That doesn't sound right.

> Sheila went shopping with me.

Yes, that's right. Now put Rachel's name back in:

> Sheila went shopping with Rachel and me.

Here's another one:

> (He or him?) and Joel won the tennis championship.

Leave out Joel's name to see what sounds right.

> Him won the tennis championship.

That doesn't sound right.

> He won the tennis championship.

Yes, that's right. Now put Joel's name back in:

> He and Joel won the tennis championship.

Use the same process if the sentence has two pronouns:

> (Her or she?) and (I or me?) decorated the room.

Leave out the second set of pronouns to see which word sounds right in the first set.

>   Her decorated the room.

That doesn't sound right.

>   She decorated the room.

That's right. Now you can choose the second pronoun by leaving out the first one:

>   Me decorated the room.

That doesn't sound right.

>   I decorated the room.

That's right. Now put them both together:

>   She and I decorated the room.

Exercise 6.1 Pronoun Case

Circle the correct pronoun. Check your answers on page 333.

1. The first-place prize in the school's robot contest went to Eric and (I – me).

2. Cecilia and (I – me) took turns driving home for Spring Break.

3. Mark invited (I – me) to play golf with (he – him) and Julian.

4. (She – Her) and Patty spent all day stripping wallpaper.

5. Be sure to call (we – us) as soon as you hear from (they – them).

6. (Him – He) and (her – she) decided to go to Hawaii for their honeymoon.

7. I know that (him – he) and (her – she) will have a wonderful trip.

8. Martha is coming over this afternoon to help Emily and (I – me) clean out the attic.

9. Nothing could have prepared (they – them) for the surprise when (they – them) won the lottery.

10. On Thanksgiving, (we – us) all go to Grandma's house to eat the wonderful meal (her – she) and Grandpa prepared.

Pronoun Agreement

What's wrong with this sentence?

John went rock climbing, and she pulled a muscle.

John is a man and doesn't want to be called *she.*

John went rock climbing, and they pulled a muscle.

John is one person, and the word *they* makes him sound like more than one.

A pronoun needs to **agree with** or match its antecedent. It needs to agree in terms of gender (John is a man; don't call him *she*), and it needs to agree in terms of number (John is one person; don't call him *they*).

Usually we choose the correct pronoun easily. But in certain tricky sentences, people often make a mistake.

Singular Indefinite Pronouns

everyone	someone	anyone	no one
everybody	somebody	anybody	nobody
each	either	neither	

These pronouns are called indefinite because they don't refer to a specific person. Most importantly, they are all singular.

It seems as if the word *everyone* would be plural because it refers to a lot of people. But *everyone* refers to one group of people.

If you replace one of these words with another pronoun, you must use a singular pronoun such as *he* or *she*, not the plural pronouns *they* or *their*.

You will hear people replace a singular indefinite pronoun with the plural words *they* or *their* all the time:

> Everyone sneezes when *they* have a cold.
> Somebody left *their* lights on.
> Did anybody lose *their* keys?

Even though these sentences sound fine, they are really not correct.

The following sentences are correct:

> Everyone sneezes when *he or she* has a cold.
> Somebody left *his or her* lights on.
> Did anybody lose *his or her* keys?

Perhaps the reason we have become so accustomed to using *they* and *their* is that *he or she* and *his or her* can sound awkward.

Here are three ways to write a smoother sentence and still use the correct pronouns:

First Method

If the indefinite pronoun is referring only to men or women, you can use just the masculine or feminine pronoun.

> Coach speaking to NFL football players:
> "Everybody should wear *his* red uniform."

> Leader speaking to a Girl Scout troop:
> "Anyone who wants to go should sign *her* name on the list."

Second Method

Keep the word *they* or *their* but replace the singular indefinite pronoun with a plural word, such as *people*.

Incorrect: Everyone sneezes when they have a cold
Correct: People sneeze when they have a cold.

Third Method

Revise the sentence to avoid the problem altogether.

Incorrect: Somebody left their lights on.
Correct: There is a red van in the parking lot with its lights on.

Incorrect: Did anybody lose their keys?
Correct: We found a set of keys in the break room.

Good news . . .

The rules about this are shifting. Some grammar books are starting to allow the use of **they** with singular indefinite pronouns. Until the time when everyone agrees to the new style, it's best to follow the traditional rule.

Pronouns with Compound Antecedents

Sometimes one pronoun can replace two names. When the two names are joined by *and*, the pronoun should be plural.

Pam brushed *her* teeth.
Pam and Sue brushed *their* teeth.

Bill washed *his* car.
Bill and Mike washed *their* cars.

When the two names are joined by *or* or *nor*, the pronoun should match the name closest to it in the sentence.

Tom will bring *his* guitar.
Either Tom or Tim will bring *his* guitar.

The scouts couldn't find *their* way.
The leader couldn't find *his* way.
Neither the scouts nor the leader could find *his* way.
Neither the leader nor the scouts could find *their* way.

As you can see, the last two sentences are essentially the same. The only difference is which antecedent is closest to the pronoun.

Try these and then check your answers below:

Max and Sam rode (his – their) bikes to the store.

Neither Max nor Sam brought (his – their) money.

Either my boyfriend or his roommates will give up (his – their) Saturday to help me move.

Let's look at the first sentence:

> Max and Sam rode (his – their) bikes to the store.

What is the antecedent for this pronoun? *Max and Sam.*

Because we have the word *and* between the two names, we need to use the plural pronoun *their.*

> Max and Sam rode *their* bikes to the store.

Trick: If you know the antecedent is plural, but you're still not sure which pronoun to choose, try replacing the antecedent with the plural word *they.*

> *They* rode *their* bikes to the store.

Here's the second sentence:

> Neither Max nor Sam brought (his – their) money.

What is the antecedent? *Max nor Sam.*

Because the word *nor* comes between the names, match the pronoun to the name that is closest to the pronoun: *Sam.*

> Sam brought *his* money.
> Neither Max nor Sam brought *his* money.

Trick: If you know the antecedent is singular, but you're still not sure which pronoun to choose, try replacing the antecedent with the singular word *he.*

He brought *his* money.

Here's the third sentence:

> Either my boyfriend or his roommates will give up
> (his – their) Saturday to help me move.

What is the antecedent? *My boyfriend or his roommates.*

Because the word *or* comes between the names, match the pronoun to the name that is closest to the pronoun: *roommates.*

> His roommates will give up *their* Saturday.

> Either my boyfriend or his roommates will give up
> *their* Saturday to help me move.

Pronouns Separated from Their Antecedents

Words that come in between the antecedent and the pronoun might cause you to choose the wrong pronoun.

> One of the tightrope walkers lost her balance.

Here the antecedent is *one.* One lost her balance. But the prepositional phrase *of the tightrope walkers* might throw you off. You might match the pronoun to *walkers:*

> One of the tightrope walkers lost their balance.

Putting parentheses around prepositional phrases can help you find the correct antecedent.

> One (of the tightrope walkers) lost *her* balance.
> Two (of the tightrope walkers) lost *their* balance.

Remember: A **preposition** is a word that tells what a cat can do with a chair: in, under, over, beside, etc.

A **prepositional phrase** is a group of words that starts with a preposition and then has a couple more words to complete the idea. For more details, see page 25.

Exercise 6.2 Pronoun Agreement

Underline the antecedent and circle the correct pronoun. Check your answers on page 334.

1. Everybody should pack (his/her – their) suitcase before going to breakfast.

2. Sylvia and I got an early start on (her – our) holiday shopping.

3. Both Bill and Roger installed satellite dishes on (his – their) roofs.

4. Neither Bill nor Roger fell off (his – their) roof.

5. Two of the boys forgot (his – their) backpacks.

6. All employees must submit (his/her – their) expense reports by Friday.

7. Someone left (her – their) purse in the conference room.

8. Neither the professor nor the students could believe (his/her – their) eyes when the lab rat escaped.

9. Anyone who answers (his/her – their) cell phone during class will be counted absent.

10. One of the girls fell and skinned (her – their) knee.

Exercise 6.3 Pronoun Agreement

Underline the antecedent and circle the correct pronoun. Check your answers on page 334.

1. All students must pay (his/her – their) library fines by the end of the semester.

2. Both Sheila and Cindy got (her – their) hair done for graduation.

3. One of the students left (his/her – their) flash drive in the computer lab.

4. Everyone can pick up (his/her – their) paycheck on Friday.

5. Someone left (his – their) football helmet and pads in the locker room.

6. Three of the kids left (his/her – their) permission slips at home.

7. Both Cody and Dustin were late for (his – their) 8:00 classes.

8. Neither Cody nor Dustin heard (his – their) alarm clock.

9. Anyone who brings cookies to class will get extra credit on (his/her – their) quiz.

10. Either the coach or the players will tell the newscaster (his – their) thoughts about the game.

Subject–Verb Agreement

Just as a pronoun needs to agree with its antecedent, the subject and the verb of a sentence must agree with or match each other.

The rules for subject–verb agreement are identical to the rules for pronoun agreement.

Singular subjects take singular verbs:

<u>Max</u> <u>eats</u> candy.   <u>Sue</u> <u>eats</u> candy.
<u>He</u> <u>eats</u> candy.   <u>She</u> <u>eats</u> candy.

All these subjects are singular, just one person, and the verb *eats* sounds right.

Now let's look at some plural subjects that take plural verbs:

<u>Max</u> and <u>Sue</u> <u>eat</u> candy.   <u>They</u> <u>eat</u> candy.

With plural subjects, the verb *eat* sounds right.

Usually it is easy to choose the verb that will agree with its subject, but certain tricky situations can give writers trouble, and these are the same situations we learned about for pronoun agreement.

Hooray! One type of tricky situation that we WON'T have to deal with here is singular indefinite pronouns. Writers automatically use a singular verb with these subjects:

> Everyone **eats** candy.
> No one **eats** candy.

Subject–Verb Agreement with Compound Subjects

Sometimes two subjects share one verb. When the two subjects are joined by *and*, the subject is plural.

> <u>Bill</u> <u>washes</u> his car.
> <u>Tom</u> <u>washes</u> his car.
> <u>Bill</u> *and* <u>Tom</u> <u>wash</u> their cars.

When the two subjects are joined by *or* or *nor,* the verb should match the subject closest to it in the sentence:

> <u>Sam</u> <u>mows</u> my lawn every weekend.
> <u>Kevin</u> <u>mows</u> my lawn every weekend.
> Either <u>Sam</u> *or* <u>Kevin</u> <u>mows</u> my lawn every weekend.

> The <u>scouts</u> <u>were</u> not lost.
> The <u>leader</u> <u>was</u> not lost.
> Neither the <u>scouts</u> *nor* the <u>leader</u> <u>was</u> lost.
> Neither the <u>leader</u> *nor* the <u>scouts</u> <u>were</u> lost.

As you can see, the last two sentences are essentially the same. The only difference is which subject is closest to the verb.

Try these and then check your answers below:

> Justin and Patrick (go – goes) to every home game.
>
> Neither Joan nor Deirdre (drinks – drink) coffee.
>
> Either Jasmine or her sisters (visits – visit) Grandma once a week.

Let's look at the first sentence:

> Justin and Patrick (go – goes) to every home game.

What is the subject for this verb? *Justin and Patrick.*

Because we have the word *and* between the two names, the subject is plural:

> <u>Justin</u> and <u>Patrick</u> <u>go</u> to every home game.

Trick: If you know the subject is plural, replace the names with the plural word *they*. Then you can hear which verb sounds right:

> <u>They</u> <u>go</u> to every home game.

Here's the second sentence:

> Neither Joan nor Deirdre (drinks – drink) coffee.

What is the subject? *Joan nor Deirdre.* Because the word *nor* comes between the two names, match the verb to the subject that is closest to it: *Deirdre.*

Deirdre <u>drinks</u> coffee.

Neither Joan nor <u>Deirdre</u> <u>drinks</u> coffee.

Trick: If you know the subject is singular, replace the name with the singular word *he* or *she*. Then you can hear which verb sounds right:

<u>She</u> <u>drinks</u> coffee.

Here's the third sentence:

Either Jasmine or her sisters (visits – visit) Grandma once a week.

What is the subject? *Jasmine or her sisters.*

Because the word *or* comes between the subjects, match the verb with the subject that is closest to it: *sisters.*

<u>Sisters</u> <u>visit</u> Grandma once a week.

Either Jasmine or her <u>sisters</u> <u>visit</u> Grandma once a week.

Subjects Separated from the Verbs

Words that come in between the subject and the verb might cause you to choose the wrong verb.

Every day <u>one</u> of the football players <u>falls</u> down.

Here the subject is one—one falls down. But the prepositional phrase *of the football players* might cause you to match the verb to *players:*

> Every day <u>one</u> of the football players <u>fall</u> down.

A word in a prepositional phrase will not be the subject. Putting parentheses around the prepositional phrase can help you find the correct subject.

> <u>One</u> (of the football players) <u>falls</u> down.
> <u>Three</u> (of the football players) <u>fall</u> down.

Remember: A **preposition** is a word that tells what a cat can do with a chair: in, under, over, beside, etc.

A **prepositional phrase** is a group of words that starts with a preposition and then has a couple more words to complete the idea. For more details, see page 25.

Exercise 6.4 Subject–Verb Agreement

Underline the subject; then circle the correct verb. Check your answers on page 335.

1. Jennifer and Nicole (meets – meet) at the Suds-n-Bubbles Laundromat every Monday to wash their clothes.

2. Either Jennifer or Nicole (brings – bring) magazines to read while the clothes are washing.

3. All of Aunt Sadie's prize rose bushes (was – were) completely covered with aphids.

4. One of the rose bushes (was – were) still blooming, however.

5. Neither the employees nor the manager (knows – know) how to install a new roll of paper into the cash register.

6. Red Lobster and Olive Garden (is – are) my favorite restaurants.

7. Neither Red Lobster nor Olive Garden (takes – take) reservations.

8. Olive Garden, one of the best Italian restaurants, (serves – serve) great spaghetti.

9. Red Lobster, which has a huge tank full of lobsters, (offers – offer) fresh seafood.

10. Both Red Lobster and Olive Garden (has – have) wonderful desserts.

Exercise 6.5 Subject–Verb Agreement

Underline the subject; then circle the correct verb. Check your answers on page 335.

1. Megan and her friends (works – work) at Starbucks.

2. Either Megan or her friends (takes – take) orders from the customers.

3. Neither Megan nor the other employees
   (wants – want) to take out the trash.

4. Megan, the newest of the employees, (has – have) to
   do this nasty job.

5. The dumpster, which is in an alley full of trash cans,
   (smells – smell) terrible.

6. Jasmine, one of Megan's co-workers, (gives – give)
   Megan a sympathetic smile.

7. Before Megan got hired, Jasmine (was – were) the
   one taking out the trash.

8. Megan and her friends (enjoys – enjoy) preparing
   the drinks.

9. The coffee and tea (smells – smell) wonderful.

10. One of Megan's favorite drinks (is – are) a skinny
    mocha.

Irregular Verbs

As you learned in Chapter 1, the verb shows the time or tense of
the sentence, so we can find verbs by changing the time/tense of
the sentence and listening for the word that changes. Most English verbs follow a regular pattern when they change:

> *Yesterday* I walked to the store.

> *Every day* I walk to the store.

> *Tomorrow* I will walk to the store.

Yesterday <u>you</u> <u>parked</u> the car.

Every day <u>you</u> <u>park</u> the car.

Tomorrow <u>you</u> <u>will park</u> the car.

Yesterday <u>they</u> <u>washed</u> the dishes.

Every day <u>they</u> <u>wash</u> the dishes.

Tomorrow <u>they</u> <u>will wash</u> the dishes.

It's easy to see the pattern these verbs follow when they change. Verbs that follow this pattern are called **regular verbs**.

One Exception . . .

If the subject is the name of one person or thing (or the word he, she, or it) the every day form adds an S on the end:
Every day Ryan walks to the store.
Every day Karen parks the car.
Every day the dishwasher washes the dishes.

Past Participles

Look at these sentences:

I have walked to the store every day for a month.
You have parked the car too close to the fire hydrant.
They have washed the dishes since we bought the
groceries.

By adding the helping verb HAVE in front of the main verb, we can create more subtle tenses than the standard past, present, and future.

Since regular verbs follow a regular pattern when they change, writers don't usually have trouble choosing the correct verb.

English also has about two hundred irregular verbs. These words don't follow the normal pattern when they change, so they can be more difficult to use.

If you learn to follow a Verb Chart, you can always use the right form of the verb in your sentences.

Let's start by looking at a Verb Chart of regular verbs:

Base Form	Past Tense	Past Participle
walk	walked	walked
park	parked	parked
wash	washed	washed

To write a sentence in present tense, use the base form of the verb:

Every day we WALK to the store.

To write a sentence in past tense, use the past tense form of the verb:

Yesterday we WALKED to the store.

To write a sentence in future tense, use WILL with the base form of the verb:

Tomorrow we WILL WALK to the store.

To write a sentence with a past participle, use HAVE, HAD, or HAS with the past participle form of the verb:

We HAVE WALKED to the store every day for a month.
Juan HAD PARKED the car before he noticed the handicapped sign.
Tina HAS WASHED her hands ten times today.

Now that we see how the verb chart works, let's try a chart of some irregular verbs.

Base Form	Past Tense	Past Participle
eat	ate	eaten
do	did	done
go	went	gone

To write a sentence in present tense, use the base form of the verb:

Every day I EAT kale.
Every day I DO fifty pushups.
Every day I GO to the gym.

To write a sentence in past tense, use the past tense form of the verb:

> Yesterday I ATE kale.
> Yesterday I DID fifty push ups.
> Yesterday I WENT to the gym.

To write a sentence in future tense, use WILL with the base form of the verb:

> Tomorrow I WILL EAT kale.
> Tomorrow I WILL DO fifty pushups.
> Tomorrow I WILL GO to the gym.

To write a sentence with a past participle, use HAVE, HAD, or HAS with the past participle form of the verb:

> I HAVE EATEN kale every day for a month.
> I HAD DONE fifty pushups before I even broke a sweat.
> I HAVE GONE to the gym already today.
> She HAS EATEN a raw foods diet for the past week.

Note: It's okay to put a word between the two verbs:

> I HAVE already GONE to the gym today.
> I HAD never EATEN kale before I started Cross Fit.

Common Irregular Verbs		
Base Form	Past Tense	Past Participle
beat	beat	beaten
become	became	become
begin	began	begun
bite	bit	bitten
break	broke	broken
bring	brought	brought
buy	bought	bought
choose	chose	chosen
come	came	come
do	did	done
draw	drew	drawn
drink	drank	drunk
drive	drove	driven
eat	ate	eaten
fall	fell	fallen
fly	flew	flown
forget	forgot	forgotten
get	got	gotten
give	gave	given
go	went	gone

Common Irregular Verbs, continued		
grow	grew	grown
have	had	had
hide	hid	hidden
know	knew	known
lose	lost	lost
make	made	made
ride	rode	ridden
run	ran	run
see	saw	seen
sing	sang	sung
sink	sank	sunk
sleep	slept	slept
steal	stole	stolen
swim	swam	swum
swing	swung	swung
take	took	taken
teach	taught	taught
throw	threw	thrown
wear	wore	worn
write	wrote	written

Exercise 6.6 – Using Irregular Verbs

Use the Chart of Irregular Verbs to write sentences in the different tenses. Use a different verb for each sentence. Check your answers on page 336.

Example: Every day I . . . choose what clothes to wear.

1. Every day I . . .
2. Yesterday you . . .
3. Tomorrow they . . .
4. We HAVE . . .
5. Every day they . . .
6. Yesterday we . . .
7. Tomorrow I . . .
8. I HAD . . .
9. She HAS . . .
10. They HAVE . . .

Mistakes to Avoid . . .

#1) Use verbs that are on the chart; don't invent your own verbs.

I went to a potluck party, and I brang a cake.

Brang is not on the chart. Use **brought** instead.

The chart in this book doesn't have every irregular verb, so if you want to check a word that is not on the chart, you can look in a dictionary.

#2) Only use a Past Participle with the word HAVE, HAD, or HAS.

They done a good job.

Done is a Past Participle. It shouldn't be used alone. There are two correct ways of writing this sentence:

They did a good job.
They HAVE done a good job.

Exercise 6.7 – Correcting Mistakes with Irregular Verbs

Some of these sentences have a verb that is not on the chart. Replace it with the correct word from the chart. Other sentences have a Past Participle used alone. Add HAVE, HAD, or HAS in front of the Past Participle or change the Past Participle to the Past Tense form of the verb. Check your answers on page 336.

1. The dog bited the mail carrier.

2. He grown so much since last year.

3. The catcher throwed the ball to first base.

4. Jill come over for dinner last night.

5. They taken too many breaks today.

6. The batter swang at the ball but missed it.

7. Jamie and Max gone to the movies.

8. Mike gotted a ticket for speeding.

9. Bill teached his daughter to ride a bike.

10. The athletes drunk lots of water to stay hydrated.

The Most Irregular of all the Irregular Verbs

The verb TO BE is really irregular. It changes for different times like other verbs, but it also changes for different subjects.

TO BE

	Every day	Yesterday	Tomorrow	Past Participle
I	am	was	will be	have been
You	are	were	will be	have been
He/She/It	is	was	will be	has been
We	are	were	will be	have been
You all	are	were	will be	have been
They	are	were	will be	have been

Exercise 6.8 – Fixing Mistakes with the Verb TO BE

Use the chart above to find and correct the mistakes in these sentences. For some of the sentences, there is more than one way to fix the mistake. Check your answers on page 337.

1. They was at the house.

2. She be a nurse.

3. You all been watching TV for three hours.

4. I is too tired to mow the grass.

5. You was at work.

6. They be too noisy.

7. I has been waiting for an hour.

8. You is the best player on the team.

9. He been working on the car.

10. We was so glad to get home before the storm came.

Chapter Seven

✧

Powerful Writing

This chapter gets into smaller details for making your writing more powerful. If your papers have problems with misplaced or dangling modifiers, you could be writing something funny that you didn't intend to say. We will also cover passive voice, wordiness, and parallel structure. These problems are easy to fix once you become aware of them.

Modifiers

A **modifier** is a word or group of words that describes or gives details.

> I have a red car.

Here the modifier is the word *red* which is describing the car. Different languages have different rules about where the modifier needs to go. The French and Spanish languages both put the modifier after the word being described:

J'ai une voiture rouge.
Yo tengo un carro rojo.
I have a car red.

In English, the modifier usually goes before the word being described. Most of the time we automatically put the modifier in the correct place. Two kinds of mistakes that writers may make are **misplaced modifiers** and **dangling modifiers.**

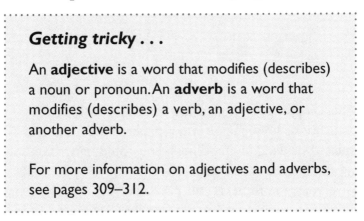

Getting tricky . . .

An **adjective** is a word that modifies (describes) a noun or pronoun. An **adverb** is a word that modifies (describes) a verb, an adjective, or another adverb.

For more information on adjectives and adverbs, see pages 309–312.

Misplaced Modifiers

A modifier placed too far away from the word it is trying to modify is called a **misplaced modifier.** You may have heard this joke from the movie *Mary Poppins*:

> I know a man with a wooden leg named Smith.
> Really? And what is the name of his other leg?

If the modifier *named Smith* is too far away from the word it is trying to modify—*man*—the sentence sounds as if his leg was named Smith.

Rearrange the words so that the modifier is closer to the word it is really modifying:

> I know a man named Smith with a wooden leg.

A **split infinitive** is a particular kind of misplaced modifier. An infinitive is the word *to* followed by a verb. Don't put any words in between the *to* and the verb.

I try *to* **always** *tell* the truth.	split infinitive
I always try *to tell* the truth.	correct
Be sure *to* **never** *break* a promise.	split infinitive
Be sure never *to break* a promise.	correct
Never break a promise.	correct

The times they are a-changin'...

The rule about split infinitives is fading away. Most grammar books don't even mention it anymore.

For more on infinitives, see page 291.

Dangling Modifiers

A **dangling modifier** occurs when the word that the modifier is trying to modify does not even appear in the sentence.

> As a young girl, her father taught her to climb trees.

The modifier is *as a young girl,* but who was a young girl? We don't have a girl's name in this sentence. It sounds as if her father used to be a young girl.

Revise this sentence carefully. It is not enough to say

> As a young girl, Sally's father taught her to climb trees.

This still sounds as if *as a young girl* is modifying *father.* Here are two correct versions:

> As a young girl, Sally climbed trees with her father.
> When Sally was a young girl, her father taught her to climb trees.

Exercise 7.1 Misplaced and Dangling Modifiers

Rewrite these sentences to solve the modifier problems.

Check your answers on page 337.

1. I loaned my wool sweater to Jackie with the red stripes.

2. To save electricity, remember to always turn down the thermostat when you leave the house.

3. The museum curator showed the new painting to the guests hanging on the wall.

4. Walking quickly, the convenience store is about ten minutes away.

5. The doctor suggested a new treatment for my in-grown toenail that is painless.

6. Patrick promised to never leave the milk out overnight again.

7. Sara ordered a bagel from the waitress with cream cheese.

8. Eating tacos, the salsa dripped all over my hands.

9. While studying for my history exam, my roommate turned on the tv.

10. The dentist told Kevin to always floss his teeth.

Passive vs. Active Voice

Remember—To find the verb in a sentence, say *yesterday, every day,* and *tomorrow* at the beginning of the sentence and then listen for the word that changes.

> *Yesterday* the bank **was robbed** by Felix.
> *Every day* the bank **is robbed** by Felix.
> *Tomorrow* the bank **will be robbed** by Felix.

To find the subject, ask "Who or what performed the verb?"

> Who or what was robbed by Felix? *bank*
> The <u>bank</u> <u>was robbed</u> by Felix.

See Chapter 1 for more details on finding verbs and subjects.

Getting tricky . . .

In the sentence about Felix, **was robbed** is the verb even though the word **robbed** didn't change when we changed the time. For practical purposes it works just fine to mark only the word that actually changes: **was.**

If you want to delve in and learn about helping verbs and verb phrases, see page 288–290.

Passive voice is when the subject of the sentence is not the person who actually did the verb.

The bank was robbed by Felix.

The verb is *was robbed.* To find the subject, we ask, "Who or what was robbed?" The answer, *bank,* is the subject.

Now ask yourself, "Did the subject actually do the verb? Did the bank do the robbing?" No. Who actually did the robbing? *Felix.*

But *Felix* is not the subject of the sentence. That's why this sentence is in **passive voice.**

Passive voice is not grammatically incorrect, but it sounds weak. It's usually best to use active voice when possible.

Turning a passive sentence into **active voice** is easy: just move the words around so that the person who actually did the verb is the subject:

<u>Felix</u> <u>robbed</u> the bank.

Let's try another sentence.

The <u>juice</u> <u>was spilled</u> by Susan.

The verb is *was spilled*. "Who or what was spilled by Susan?" The answer, *juice*, is the subject.

"Did the subject actually do the verb? Did the juice spill anything?" No. "Who spilled it?" *Susan*

The active voice version of this sentence looks like this:

<u>Susan</u> <u>spilled</u> the juice.

Here's one more example:

The <u>award</u> <u>was won</u> by Serena.

The verb is *was won*. "Who or what was won by Serena?"

The answer, *award*, is the subject.

"Did the award win anything?" No. "Who actually won it?" *Serena.*

The active voice version of this sentence looks like this:

<u>Serena</u> <u>won</u> the award.

Sometimes passive voice is the best choice. What if you don't know who robbed the bank?

The <u>bank</u> <u>was robbed</u>!!

This is passive voice because the subject *bank* did not actually do the robbing. You could still write this sentence as active voice by saying

<u>Somebody</u> <u>robbed</u> the bank!!

Exercise 7.2 Passive Voice

Rewrite each sentence in active voice. If the passive sentence does not say who performed the verb, use *someone* as the subject in your active voice sentence. Check your answers on page 339.

EXAMPLE: The pool was cleaned last week.

Someone cleaned the pool last week.

1. The brownies were eaten by Sandy.

2. King Louis XVI was beheaded in Paris in 1793.

3. The dishes were washed by George.

4. A buried treasure chest was dug up by the pirate.

5. The incorrect statistics were released by a member of the committee.

6. Three priceless paintings were found in a storage unit.

7. The new construction project was approved by the board.

8. The faulty valve had been inspected two months earlier.

9. Tickets will be taken by the ushers.

10. The new movie will be released on October 1.

Avoiding Wordiness

Writing that uses many more words than really needed is called **wordy**:

> After the end of the final curtain call, we exited the theater, went outside, and walked down the sidewalk to a little, small, cozy restaurant café.

Some of the words in this sentence repeat what has already been said: *little, small, cozy*. Other words aren't needed. A shorter version is easier to read and more powerful because it expresses the same idea with fewer words:

> When the play ended, we walked to a cozy restaurant.

Many writers will use unnecessary words when they write a rough draft because they are trying to figure out what they want to say. When you revise your rough draft, be sure to eliminate those unnecessary words.

Also, writers may use extra words in an attempt to sound formal and sophisticated. Usually it's better to say what you mean succinctly and clearly while still maintaining an appropriate level of formality.

> Due to the fact that my purse is empty and devoid of any money, either paper or coin, I must decline your invitation to the cinema movie theater and satisfy myself with watching video entertainment on my television for the present time until the occasion arises that I once again enjoy the abundance of funds for discretionary usage.

The shorter version is still formal, but it is much easier for the reader to understand:

> Unfortunately, I must decline your invitation because I do not have sufficient funds in my entertainment budget at this time.

Exercise 7.3 Revising Wordiness

Rewrite the following passage to eliminate unnecessary words and make the instructions easier to understand. One possible answer is given on page 339.

In the event that the engine of the lawn and yard mower fails to start or begin running following a quick, swift, and rapid pulling action upon the mower's starting cord, the owner of the mower who is making an attempt to bring the mower's engine into a running condition would be advised to use any of his or her fingers or thumbs to push down upon and press the mower's primer button several times in rapid succession so that upon a second attempt at pulling the cord the owner and user of the lawn and yard mower might experience increased probability of a successful outcome to a subsequent quick, swift, and rapid pull upon the mower's starting cord.

Parallel Structure

Why does the following sentence sound awkward?

Sam mowed the grass and trimming the shrubs.

This sentence tells two things that Sam did, but the two things are not presented in a parallel way: **mowed** doesn't match with **trimming.** This type of mistake is called faulty parallelism. Correct faulty parallelism by choosing words that match:

Sam mowed the grass and trimmed the shrubs.

Not Parallel	**Parallel**
Sam wants to	Sam wants to
mow the grass,	mow the grass,
trim the shrubs, and	trim the shrubs, and
raking the leaves.	rake the leaves.

Not Parallel	**Parallel**
Sam wants	Sam wants
to mow the grass,	to mow the grass,
to trim the shrubs, and	to trim the shrubs, and
raking the leaves.	to rake the leaves.

Not Parallel
Sam was
  mowing the grass,
  trimming the shrubs, and
  to rake the leaves.

Parallel
Sam was
  mowing the grass,
  trimming the shrubs, and
  raking the leaves.

Not Parallel
Sam trimmed
  the rose bushes,
  the holly bushes, and
  hydrangeas

Parallel
Sam trimmed
  the rose bushes,
  the holly bushes, and
  the hydrangea bushes.

Not Parallel
Sam trimmed
  the roses,
  the hollies, and
  the hydrangea bushes.

Parallel
Sam trimmed
  the roses,
  the hollies, and
  the hydrangeas.

Not Parallel
Sam raked
  under the trees,
  around the swingset, and
  the house.

Parallel
Sam raked
  under the trees,
  around the swingset, and
  beside the house.

Not Parallel
Sam got
  hot,
  sweaty, and
  he was thirsty.

Parallel
Sam got
  hot,
  sweaty, and
  thirsty.

Exercise 7.4 Practice with Parallel Structure

Rewrite each sentence to fix any problems with parallelism. Check your answers on page 339.

EXAMPLE:

Sally enjoys watching movies, reading books, and to go to the mall.

Sally enjoys watching movies, reading books, and *going* to the mall.

1. In the attic, I found a broken typewriter, an old suitcase, and a doll house that was dusty.

2. Scott was voted player of the year for his speed, concentration, and his ability to lead.

3. Florida is a popular vacation spot because it has theme parks, beaches, and the weather is great.

4. Jan's new job pays well, has great benefits, and she gets two weeks of vacation.

5. The mouse ran across the kitchen floor, behind the refrigerator, and there was a hole that he went into.

6. The movie was dramatic and with lots of excitement.

7. Patricia went to the grocery store, the dry cleaners, and stopped at the bank.

8. The library smelled like mildew, dust, and like old books.

9. During spring break, Jake wants to go to the beach, eat lots of seafood, and getting a tan.

10. The flight attendants were cheerful, friendly, and with smiles.

Chapter Eight

✧

Homophones

Homophone means "same sound." Homophones (also called homonyms) are words that sound the same but are spelled differently and have different meanings.

Trick: For some of these homophones, one of the words is a verb, and the other word is not a verb. To determine which word to use in your sentence, change the time or tense of the sentence by saying the three time words—yesterday, every day, and tomorrow—at the beginning of the sentence. If the word changes, that word is a verb. If the word does not change when you change the time of the sentence, use the word that is not a verb. For more information on finding verbs, turn to pages 4–9.

Example: **Accept** is a verb; **except** is not a verb.

> *Yesterday* Sue **accepted** Jill's gift.
>
> *Every day* Sue **accepts** Jill's gift.
>
> *Tomorrow* Sue **will accept** Jill's gift.

Since the word *accept* changed when we changed the time of the sentence, this word is a verb, so we use *accept* instead of except.

Yesterday Sue did all her homework **except** math.

Every day Sue does all her homework **except** math.

Tomorrow Sue will do all her homework **except** math.

In these sentences, the word **except** did not change when we changed the time. **Except** is not the verb of these sentences, so we use **except** instead of *accept*.

General Homophones

accept — I accept your apology.
Accept is a verb.

except — Joan remembered everything except her camera.
Except means leaving out something. Except is not a verb.

advice — My uncle gives me good advice.
*In **advice**, the C sounds like an S. Advice is not a verb.*

advise — I would advise you not to eat that moldy cheese.
*In **advise**, the S sounds like a Z. Advise is a verb.*

affect — The soggy field might affect the team's performance.
Affect is a verb.

effect — Jason said his daily run was having a good effect on his health.
Effect is not a verb.

For more on nouns and verbs, see pages 304 and 305.

a lot	Movie stars receive a lot of fan mail. *A lot is two separate words. A lot is not a verb.*
allot	Dad will allot me $20 per week. *Allot means give. Allot is a verb.*
already	That test was easy. I am already finished.
all ready	We were all ready to go by six o'clock. *All ready means completely prepared.*
are	We are going to the zoo. *Are is a verb.*
our	This is our house. *Our is not a verb.*
bare	I like to feel the grass under my bare feet.
bear	Lucy has a stuffed teddy bear. I can't bear to see you cry.
bored	On rainy days, little children get bored.
board	We were the last ones to board the plane. Steve cut the board in half with his saw.
break	Be careful not to break anything. Every two hours, you get a ten-minute break.
brake	Hit the brake! There's a stop sign!
buy	I will buy a new car when I finish school. *Buy is a verb.*
by	I have a night light by my bed. *By is a preposition, not a verb.*

capitol	Her office is in the state capitol building.
capital	Raleigh is the capital city of North Carolina.
coarse	Coarse sandpaper is very rough.
course	Gerry teaches the piano course. On Saturdays, the golf course is crowded.

compliment Mary's date gave her a compliment.
A compliment is a nice comment.

complement David chose a tie to complement his suit.
Complement means "go with" or "enhance."

conscience	Do you have a guilty conscience?
conscious	Jim was unconscious after the accident.
dairy	Milk is in the dairy section.
diary	Becky writes in her diary every day.
every day	Debbie makes her bed every day.
everyday	These are my everyday shoes. *Everyday as one word means ordinary or common.*
forth	The explorers went forth into the wilderness.
fourth	Elizabeth is in fourth grade.
fare	To ride the bus, you must pay a dollar fare.
fair	Divide the work equally so that it will be fair. Every fall, Scott goes to the county fair. Jill gets sunburned easily because she is fair.
herd	A group of cattle is called a herd.

heard	I just heard the good news! *Heard contains the word ear. You heard something with your ears. Heard is a verb.*
here	When will Marcus be here? Here is that CD I borrowed.
hear	I hear the music from the room next door. *Hear contains ear; you hear with your ear.* *Hear is a verb.*
horse	A cowboy rides a horse.
hoarse	Jamie yelled until her voice was hoarse.
its	The cat chased its ball. *Use its when you don't mean it is.*
it's	It's a hot day today. *It's is a contraction of it is.*

For a review of contractions, turn to page 81.

lay and lie	turn to page 158.
led	Sue led me to the surprise party.
lead	Lead is a kind of metal. In ballroom dancing, the man will lead. *For this meaning, lead is pronounced LEED.*
loose	These pants are too loose and baggy. *Loose is not a verb.*
lose	The team will lose if they don't practice harder. *Lose is a verb.*

meat	Mary doesn't eat meat; she's a vegetarian. *Meat is a noun, not a verb.*
meet	Tomorrow I will meet my new roommate. *Meet is a verb.*
no	No, I don't like tomatoes. *No is not a verb.*
know	Alex knows how to do magic tricks. *Know is a verb.*
past	History teaches stories from the past. *Past is a noun, not a verb.*
passed	Oh no! We just passed the house! Sally passed the class with a B. *Passed is a verb.*
patience	Teaching preschool requires a lot of patience.
patients	The nurse cared for five patients.
piece	May I have another piece of cake please? *Piece contains pie, like a piece of pie.*
peace	Sue enjoyed an hour of peace and quiet.
plane	Have you ever ridden on an airplane? Carpenters use a plane to shave wood.
plain	I'll have my cake plain, no ice cream. A big, grassy area is called a plain.
presents	Vanessa received five presents for Christmas.
presence	Shawn appreciated his mother's presence while he was in the hospital.
principal	Mr. Shawnessy is the principal of the school.

principle	A minister should have good principles.
rain	There is a ten percent chance of rain today.
rein	When you ride a horse, hold the reins firmly.
reign	The reign of Elizabeth I was the Golden Age.
right	At the next intersection, turn right. I believe I got all the answers right. *Right is not a verb.*
write	Denise likes to write poetry. *Write is a verb.*
rode	I rode a horse around the corral. *Rode is a verb.*
road	Look both ways before you cross the road. *Road is a noun, not a verb.*
scene	I enjoyed a beautiful scene of the ocean. A play is divided into acts and scenes.
seen	Have you seen my jacket?
sense	That theory just doesn't make any sense. I have an excellent sense of smell.
since	Since I mowed the lawn, you should trim the shrubs.
than	Zack is taller than Zoe. *Than is used for comparing.*
then	Let's wash the dishes; then we can watch tv. *Then means next.*
their	My neighbors love their new dog. *Their shows possession.*

there	There are three frogs in the pond.
	The bathrooms are over there.
	*There is the most commonly used of the three spellings. Use **there** by default if you don't mean possession or **they are**.*
they're	They're driving to Florida this summer.
	*They're is a contraction of **they are**.*

For a review of contractions, turn to page 81.

through	Let's drive through the park.
	Through is not a verb; it is a preposition meaning between or inside.
threw	The pitcher threw a curve ball.
	Threw is a verb.
to	I'm going to the store to buy some shoes.
	*To is the most commonly used of the three spellings. Use **to** by default if you don't mean a number, also, or an excessive amount.*
two	I will also buy two new dresses.
	Two means the number.
too	Is that too much to spend in one day?
	Would you like to come too?
	Too means also or an excessive amount.
waste	Don't waste electricity.
waist	The pirate wore a red sash around his waist.
wear	What should I wear today?
	Wear contains the word ear. You can wear an earring.

where	Where is my hair brush?
week	My birthday is one week from today.
weak	I do push-ups so I'll be strong, not weak.
were	We were stuck in traffic for two hours! *Were is a verb.*
we're	We're going to the movies. *We're is a contraction of we are.*
whether	I wonder whether it will rain. *Whether means if.*
weather	The weather is perfect for a picnic.
who and whom	turn to page 159.
whose	Whose turn is it to clean the bathroom? *Use whose when you don't mean who is.*
who's	Do you know who's going to be at the party? *Who's is a contraction of who is.*
your	This is your glass of lemonade. *Your means ownership, possession. Use your when you don't mean you are.*
you're	You're supposed to call after 2 p.m. *You're is a contraction of you are.*

For a review of contractions, turn to page 81.

Lay and Lie

The words *lay and lie* are tricky because their meanings are quite similar and the tenses overlap. The past tense of the verb *lie* is the same word as the present tense of the verb *lay.*

The verb *lie* means to recline your body or to be in a reclining position:

> *Every day* I **lie** down and take a nap.
> *Tomorrow* I **will lie** down and take a nap.
> *Yesterday* I **lay** down and took a nap.

> *Every day* he **lies** down and takes a nap.
> *Tomorrow* he **will lie** down and take a nap.
> *Yesterday* he **lay** down and took a nap.

> *Every day* the newspaper **is lying** on the doorstep.
> *Tomorrow* the newspaper **will be lying** on the doorstep.
> *Yesterday* the newspaper **was lying** on the doorstep.

> *Today* I **have been lying** on the couch for an hour.
> *Tomorrow* I **will have been lying** on the couch for an hour.
> *Yesterday* I **had been lying** on the couch for an hour.

The verb *lay* means to place an object:

> *Every day* I **lay** my keys on the kitchen table.
> *Tomorrow* I **will lay** my keys on the kitchen table.
> *Yesterday* I **laid** my keys on the kitchen table.

> *Every day* She **lays** her keys on the kitchen table.
> *Tomorrow* She **will lay** her keys on the kitchen table.
> *Yesterday* She **laid** her keys on the kitchen table.

Today I **am laying** my keys on the table.
Tomorrow I **will be laying** my keys on the table.
Yesterday I **was laying** my keys on the table.

Here is another way to choose between *lay and lie*: **Lay** is a transitive verb which means that it takes a direct object. **Lie** is an intransitive verb which means it does not take a direct object. See page 290 for an explanation of transitive and intransitive verbs.

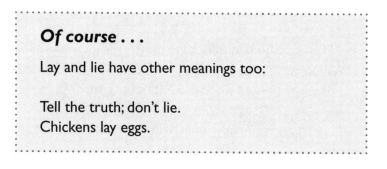

Of course . . .

Lay and lie have other meanings too:

Tell the truth; don't lie.
Chickens lay eggs.

Who and Whom

The words *who* and *whom* are really difficult. To understand the intricacies of *who* and *whom*, you would need to do an extensive study of traditional grammar which is beyond the scope of what most people need to know in order to write correctly. In fact, *whom* is disappearing from the language and is rarely used except in very formal writing.

The following method for *who* and *whom* works well in most cases.

Use *who* when you could answer the question with *she, he,* or *they*:

Who won the race?
She won the race.

The prize went to the person **who** finished first.
Who finished first?
He finished first.

Who can be calling so late at night?
They can be calling so late at night.

I forgot **who** is supposed to do the dishes tonight.
Who is supposed to do the dishes tonight?
She is supposed to do the dishes tonight.

Use *whom* when you could answer the question with *her, him,* or *them:*

The partner **whom** I was assigned to was terrible.
Whom was I assigned to?
I was assigned to **him**.

The producer is Ms. Spencer **whom** you will be working with closely.
Whom will you be working with closely?
You will be working with **her**.

Whom did the victim identify as the robber?
The victim identified **him** as the robber.

With **whom** did you hike last summer?
You hiked with **them** last summer.

Chapter Nine

✧

Sentence Types

This chapter teaches the steps for identifying the four different types of sentences: simple, compound, complex, and compound-complex.

People write all four types of sentences even though they may not know what the sentences are called. Because the smoothest, most interesting writing uses a mixture of sentences, a conscious awareness of the four types can help you improve your writing style as well as your punctuation.

Remember—An **independent clause** has a subject and a verb, and it expresses a complete idea.

> Mario hit the winning run   IC
> the weather was cold   IC

A **dependent clause** also has a subject and a verb, but it leaves the reader hanging. A dependent clause begins with a **subordinating conjunction** that changes the sound of the clause.

<u>after</u> <u>Mario</u> <u>hit</u> the winning run . . . what?   DC
<u>although</u> the <u>weather</u> <u>was</u> cold . . . what?   DC

A **phrase** is any group of words that does not have a subject and a verb.

in the morning   Ph
<u>wore</u> a blue suit   Ph

For more information on clauses, phrases, and subordinating conjunctions, see pages 21–29.

Common Subordinating Conjunctions

after	although	as	because
before	if	since	so that
that	though	till	until
unless	when	where	while

The Four Sentence Types

Phrases, dependent clauses, and independent clauses are the building blocks that we use to make the four different types of sentences.

We analyze sentence type by counting how many independent clauses and how many dependent clauses a sentence has. Phrases don't matter.

A **simple sentence** has only one clause—an independent clause. Mark simple sentences **S.**

> Josephine <u>wore</u> a purple velvet gown.
>   IC

> (At the New Year's Eve Ball), Josephine <u>wore</u> a
>   Ph   IC
> purple velvet gown (with a satin cape).
>   Ph

The second sentence is much longer because it has two phrases. But it is still a simple sentence because it has only one clause.

A **compound sentence** has two (or more) independent clauses. Mark compound sentences **CP.**

> <u>Philip</u> <u>saw</u> Josephine; <u>he</u> <u>asked</u> her to dance.
> IC   IC

> <u>Philip</u> <u>saw</u> Josephine (in her purple gown); (with a
> IC   Ph   Ph
> nervous voice) <u>he</u> <u>asked</u> her to dance.
>   IC

The second sentence is much longer because it has two phrases. But it is still a compound sentence because it has two independent clauses.

A **complex sentence** has one independent clause and one (or more) dependent clauses. It doesn't matter whether the dependent clause comes first or last. Mark complex sentences **CX.**

> <u>After</u> <u>they</u> <u>danced</u>, <u>they</u> <u>drank</u> champagne.
>   DC   IC
> <u>They</u> <u>drank</u> champagne <u>after</u> <u>they</u> <u>danced</u>.
> IC   DC

If the dependent clause comes first, put a comma after it. If the independent clause comes first, don't put a comma. See page 51 for more information.

A **compound-complex sentence** has at least three clauses. Like a complex sentence, it has at least one dependent clause. Like a compound sentence, it has two (or more) independent clauses. It doesn't matter what order the clauses are in. Mark compound-complex sentences **CPX**.

> When the ball ended, Philip took Josephine (to a
> DC   IC
> restaurant), and they dined (on truffles and caviar).
> Ph   IC   Ph

Steps for Analyzing Sentence Types

1. Double Underline the Verbs

2. Underline the Subjects

3. Count the Clauses: One clause—mark it **S for simple** More than one clause—go on to the next step

4. Are there any subordinating conjunctions? No— mark it **CP for compound** Yes—draw a wavy line under them—go on to the next step

5. How many independent clauses are there? One— mark it **CX for complex** Two or more—**CPX for compound-complex**

> **Getting tricky . . .**
>
> See pages 300–301 to learn about relative clauses that count as dependent clauses in analyzing sentence type.

Exercise 9.1 Analyzing Sentence Types

Follow the steps and identify the type for each sentence. Check your answers on page 340.

EXAMPLE: Following her junior year in college, <u>Chelsea</u> <u>traveled</u> to Europe for the summer; <u>Jordan</u> <u>remained</u> on campus. **CP**

1. After Chelsea left, Jordan found himself bored and restless.

2. He spent several days watching TV and playing video games.

3. Chelsea sent him pictures of the Globe Theatre and Big Ben, and he sent her pictures of his cactus and the empty basketball court.

4. One day Jordan walked the entire campus, discovering numerous new buildings.

5. The next day he returned to the Career Center where he found job postings and internship opportunities.

6. Chelsea, meanwhile, sent pictures of the Eiffel Tower.

7. When Jordan found a local company looking for an intern in their accounting department, he e-mailed to ask about the position; they immediately replied that they had a sudden opening.

8. The previous intern left in disgrace after he spilled coffee on the computer.

9. Jordan spent the next six weeks as an intern.

10. At the end of the summer, Chelsea had numerous adventures in Europe to share, and Jordan had an internship experience for his résumé.

Exercise 9.2 Analyzing Sentence Types

Follow the steps and identify the type for each sentence. Check your answers on page 340.

EXAMPLE: <u>Elephants</u> <u>are</u> called pachyderms; <u>this</u> <u>means</u> "thick skinned." **CP**

1. Because they eat a lot of vegetation, elephants travel long distances.

2. In just one day, an average elephant will eat over three hundred pounds of vegetation.

3. Elephants grow up to twelve feet tall, and they weigh up to fourteen hundred pounds.

4. Elephants have the largest brain of any animal; a typical elephant brain is four times as large as a human brain.

5. An elephant's trunk is very sensitive because it contains forty thousand muscles; an elephant can pick up a small coin with its trunk.

6. Although predators will kill baby elephants, adult elephants are typically safe from all predators except humans.

7. Despite their reputation for never forgetting anything, an elephant's memory is similar to a cat's memory.

8. The white elephant gift originated in ancient Asia where ordinary elephants were common, but white elephants were rare.

9. Since white elephants were sacred, the unlucky owner of a white elephant had to feed it special food and entertain the elephant's many visitors.

10. No one wanted to receive a white elephant as a gift.

Tricky Details in Analyzing Sentence Types

Compound Verbs and Subjects—Counting the clauses can be tricky if a clause has a compound verb or a compound subject or both. Consider the difference between these two sentences:

<u>Sue</u> and <u>Joe</u> <u>cooked</u> dinner and <u>washed</u> the dishes.
<u>Sue</u> <u>cooked</u> dinner, and <u>Joe</u> <u>washed</u> the dishes.

The first sentences has a compound subject (Sue and Joe) and a compound verb (cooked and washed). Both people did both things. The structure is subject – subject – verb – verb. This is just one clause!

In the second sentence the structure is different: subject – verb – subject – verb. Sue didn't wash the dishes, and Joe didn't cook. This sentence has two clauses!

Here's how you should mark these two sentences:

<u>Sue</u> and <u>Joe</u> <u>cooked</u> dinner and <u>washed</u> the dishes.   **S**

<u>Sue</u> <u>cooked</u> dinner, and <u>Joe</u> <u>washed</u> the dishes.   **CP**

False Subordinating Conjunctions

Usually it is easy to find subordinating conjunctions. You can simply look at the first word of a clause, and if that word is on the list of subordinating conjunctions, you draw a wavy line under it.

<u>After</u> <u>Jamie</u> <u>rode</u> the Zipper, her <u>stomach</u> <u>was</u> upset.
           DC   IC

In this sentence, the word *after* makes the first clause dependent:

<u>After</u> <u>Jamie</u> <u>rode</u> the Zipper . . . what happened?

The first clause depends on the second (independent) clause to finish the idea.

But the word *after* is not always a subordinating conjunction.

After riding the Zipper, <u>Jamie</u> <u>had</u> an upset stomach.
                        IC

This sentence has only one clause. Is the word *after* making the clause dependent? When you say the sentence out loud, does it sound as if you need to keep talking to finish the idea? No. This sentence sounds finished. The word *after* is not making the clause dependent, so *after* is not working as a subordinating conjunction in this sentence.

So don't rely only on your eyes to identify subordinating conjunctions. Use your ears too. If you see a word that is on the list of subordinating conjunctions, read that clause out loud to hear if it sounds unfinished. If the clause sounds unfinished, you know that it is a dependent clause and the first word of the clause is functioning as a subordinating conjunction.

Getting tricky . . .

If **after** isn't a subordinating conjunction in this sentence, what is it?

After is part of a phrase that functions as an adverb. For an explanation of adverbs, see paged 310–312.

Exercise 9.3 Tricky Sentence Types

Follow the steps to analyze these sentences. Look out for compound subjects and verbs. Before you draw any wavy lines, make sure that word is really doing the job of a subordinating conjunction. Write **S, CP, CX,** or **CPX.** Check your answers on page 341.

1. Zork and Zink were aliens from the planet Zigland.

2. Because they were scientists, they wanted to visit Earth, so they traveled nearly a million miles.

3. When they landed on Earth, they were astonished by the colors.

4. On Zigland the grass is purple, and the sky looks yellow.

5. After climbing down from their space ship, Zork and Zink went exploring.

6. They gathered plant specimens and took water samples.

7. Although they wanted to interview some animals, they failed to make sense of the animals' noises.

8. Since Zork and Zink were the size of mice, a stray cat chased and cornered them; she hoped for a new lunch meat.

9. The tiny scientists immediately beamed themselves back to their ship and took off for Zigland.

10. After returning to Zigland with their samples, they received a hero's welcome.

Common Subordinating Conjunctions

after	although	as	because
before	if	since	so that
that	though	till	until
unless	when	where	while

Chapter Ten

✧

Research Skills

Most students will need to write many different types of research papers during college. An art history professor, a chemistry professor, and a psychology professor will assign very different research papers; however, every research project will require you to use the research skills covered in this chapter.

How this Chapter is Organized

Part One: The Big Picture

How is a research paper different from an ordinary essay?

What additional tasks are involved in writing a research paper?

What skills do you need to learn in order to complete a research paper?

Part Two: Learning the Skills You Will Need

Doing Research

Paraphrasing and Summarizing

Quoting

Taking Notes

Documenting Sources with In-Text Citations and Signal Phrases

Documenting Sources with a List of Works Cited

Part Three: Using your Skills to Write a Research Paper Step-by-Step

Step 1: Doing Preliminary Research

Step 2: Developing Your Research Question

Step 3: Finding Information and Maintaining a Working Bibliography

Step 4: Taking Notes (Paraphrasing, Summarizing, and Quoting)

Step 5: Sorting Your Notes into Piles Based on the Key Words

Step 6: Rearranging Your Notes into a Skeleton Draft

Step 7: Smoothing the Skeleton Draft into a Rough Draft

Step 8: Revising

Step 9: Removing Unnecessary In-Text Citations

Step 10: Editing

Step 11: Formatting

Step 12: Finishing Your Paper and Celebrating!

Part 1: The Big Picture

Read the research paper on the following pages and consider how it is more complicated than ordinary essays. What additional tasks did the student have to perform to complete this paper?

Bradshaw 1

Tiffany Bradshaw

Professor Anders

English 111

16 April 2017

America's Renaissance Man

Most United States money displays the face of a former president: George Washington appears on the dollar bill and the quarter; Abraham Lincoln is on the five dollar bill and the penny; Thomas Jefferson is on the nickel, and Franklin Delano Roosevelt is on the dime. But the hundred dollar bill has the face of Benjamin

Franklin, a man who never held any public office. What earned
Franklin his place on the hundred dollar bill? *Encyclopedia
Britanica* argues that, although Benjamin Franklin is "best
remembered for his role in separating the American colonies from
Great Britain," politics was only one of his many interests. Noted
biographer James Dillon writes that Franklin had "an infectious
sense of wonder and curiosity" for a wide variety of topics. An
examination of Franklin's remarkable life shows that it was his
successful leadership in many different areas that made him an
important figure in American history.

Benjamin Franklin was born in Boston, Massachusetts, in 1706;
his father was a tradesman who made soap and candles. When
Franklin was ten years old, his father took him out of school to help
with the family business. Franklin found this work boring, however,
so at the age of twelve, he began an apprenticeship in the printing
shop of his older brother, James. Franklin became interested in
writing, but James refused to publish his little brother's work, so
Franklin sent articles to James under the pen name Mrs. Silence
Dogood. Readers loved the articles, but when James found out that
they had really been written by his brother, James became very
angry. Consequently, Franklin left the print shop in Boston and
eventually moved to Philadelphia ("Benjamin").

According to *Bio,* Franklin worked at several different jobs in
Philadelphia including bookkeeping, shop keeping, and printing.

Finally, in 1728, he and a partner started their own print shop ("Benjamin"). Around 1729 he began publishing a newspaper called the *Pennsylvania Gazette,* and in 1732 he started a series of magazines called *Poor Richard's Almanac.* He used the pen name Richard Saunders and wrote articles "praising prudence [wisdom], industry [hard work], and honesty" ("Franklin"). These articles use a humorous tone to offer common-sense advice to readers. In one article titled "Reasons to Choose an Older Mistress," Franklin describes eight reasons why it is better to date an older woman than a young woman. His final argument is "... they are so grateful!!" (qtd. in Isaacson 125). *Bio* points out that Franklin did not follow his own advice, however, for he married a young woman named Deborah Read. They were married for forty-four years and had three children.

In 1748 Franklin stopped working at the newspaper and focused on science ("Franklin"). Dillon writes that Franklin believed his experiments and inventions "could advance the course of scientific and philosophical knowledge." Some of Franklin's many inventions include bifocal glasses, the glass harmonica, and the free-standing wood stove. His famous experiment of flying a kite in a thunderstorm helped him understand electricity, and this led to his invention of the lightning rod and a battery for storing electricity (Dillon). Franklin was now a leading citizen of Philadelphia, and he used his position to start several projects for the benefit of others. He

Bradshaw 4

started the first fire department, a free lending library, and a school

that later became the University of Pennsylvania ("Franklin").

Britanica details Franklin's work as a diplomat between 1757

and 1775. Franklin was selected to represent the interests of

Pennsylvania and several other colonies in England, so he spent

several years living in London working to promote the colonies'

interests with the English government. In 1775, seeing that there

could soon be a war between England and the colonies, Franklin

returned home. *Bio* describes how Franklin played an important

role in the fight for independence and the development of a new

government for the young United States of America. He served as

a delegate to the Second Continental Congress, was one of the five

men who wrote the Declaration of Independence, and was one of

the thirteen who wrote the Articles of Confederation

("Benjamin"). At the beginning of the Revolutionary War,

Franklin travelled to France to ask the French government to help

the colonies by providing money and military assistance

("Franklin"). In 1783, after the Revolutionary War ended,

Franklin and several other diplomats negotiated the peace treaty

with England ("Benjamin").

    According to *Bio*, in 1785 Franklin served as Pennsylvania's

representative to the Constitutional Convention where he played

an important role in writing the Constitution and electing George

Washington as the first president. Isaacson suggests that writing the

Constitution was a difficult task and the members had different opinions about how the new government should be set up. Anger and arguing began to replace calm discussion. After months of work and debate, some of the representatives still did not want to sign the new Constitution. Franklin's wisdom and humility can be seen in this excerpt of the closing speech he made to the members of the Constitutional Convention.

> I confess that I do not entirely approve this Constitution at present, but sir, I am not sure I shall never approve it: for having lived long, I have experienced many instances of being obliged, by better information or fuller consideration, to change opinions even on important subjects, which I once thought right, but found to be otherwise. It is therefore that the older I grow the more apt I am to doubt my own judgment, and to pay more respect to the judgment of others.... I cannot help expressing a wish, that every member of the convention, who may still have objections to it, would with me on this occasion doubt a little of his own infallibility, and to make manifest our unanimity, put his name to this instrument. (qtd. in Isaacson 364–65)

After the adoption of the Constitution, Franklin continued to work for the betterment of society. He worked to end slavery by serving as president for the Pennsylvania Society for Promoting the Abolition of Slavery ("Benjamin").

In his later years, Franklin received many honors. Dillon describes Franklin as achieving "rock star status in Europe and some quarters of the United States." In France, Franklin was so highly regarded that his supporters hired a famous sculptor to make a statue of him. The inscription at the bottom of the statue reads, "He snatched the lightning from the sky and the scepter [royal staff] from tyrants" (Dillon). Franklin was awarded honorary degrees from several prestigious universities including Harvard, Yale, Oxford, and the University of England. He died in 1790 at the age of eighty-four after suffering from gout and other illnesses for several years ("Benjamin").

Franklin became an essential figure in American history through his writing, his inventions, his diplomacy, his public service, and his wisdom in working with others to create a new government. Dillon points out that Franklin's example clearly inspired other Americans, for "when Davy Crocket died at the Alamo in 1836, almost fifty years after Franklin's death, the book he had in his pocket was not the Bible, but a copy of Franklin's *Autobiography*." *Bio* describes Franklin as "a man who never finished school but shaped his life through abundant reading and experience, a strong moral compass and an unflagging commitment to civic duty, and an overall wit, good humor and integrity." Clearly, Franklin deserves his place on the hundred dollar bill.

Works Cited

"Benjamin Franklin." *Bio.* A&E Television Networks, 17 Nov. 2015,

www.biography.com/people/benjamin-franklin-9301234.

Dillon, James J. "Benjamin Franklin: A Wonder-Based Approach to Life

and Learning." *Encounter*, vol. 22 no. 4, 2009, pp. 38-47. Ebsco Host,

www.connection.ebscohost.com/c/articles/49007048/benjamin-

franklin-wonder-based-approach-life-learning.

"Franklin, Benjamin." *Encyclopedia Britannica.* 1998.

Isaccson, Walter. *A Benjamin Franklin Reader.* Simon and Schuster, 2003.

What Additional Tasks Are Needed for Writing a Research Paper?

Besides the usual tasks required for writing any essay, a research paper involves three extra tasks:

#1 **Do research** to find the information that you will need.

#2 **Take notes** as you read your sources.
Taking notes requires two skills:

> 1) **Paraphrasing/Summarizing:** rewriting the information in your own words
>
> 2) **Quoting:** copying some of the words from the source

#3 **Document** your information.
Documenting means telling your reader where your information came from. You must document your sources in two ways:

> 1) Use **in-text citations** (also called parenthetical notes) and **signal phrases** throughout the essay.
>
> 2) Include a **list of Works Cited** on a separate page at the end of your paper.

Now that we've looked at the big picture, we can start learning the skills you will need to complete each of these tasks.

Different Styles for Documenting Research

There are several different formats a writer can use to document the sources in a research paper. This book shows the MLA (Modern Language Association) style which is used in English and most humanities classes.

APA (American Psychological Association) is another popular style which is often used for science and social science classes. Many history professors prefer Chicago or Turabian style.

These styles are different in small ways, but they all have the same purpose: to tell the reader where the information came from. Once you understand MLA documentation, it is not too difficult to switch to a different format. You can look in a reference book or use an online source and follow the examples given for that style.

Plagiarism

Plagiarism means putting your name on something that you didn't really write. Extreme plagiarism would be taking an entire essay off the internet and putting your name on it. A more common type of plagiarism happens when students aren't careful with their paraphrasing, quoting, and documentation. The consequences for all types of plagiarism are often severe. Follow the guidelines in this chapter for paraphrasing, summarizing, quoting, and documenting, and you will be able to write a strong paper without plagiarism.

Part 2: Learning the Skills You Will Need

First Skill: Doing Research

If you have any trouble finding sources in your library, don't hesitate to ask for help. The library staff and reference librarians are there to help students find the materials they need.

Thinking Ahead: Keeping a Working Bibliography

As you do research, create a **working bibliography.** A working bibliography is just a rough draft of your Works Cited page. Whenever you find a source that looks useful, list that source on your working bibliography. This will ensure that you have all the information that you will need later when you do the final draft of your Works Cited page. Nothing is more frustrating that having to go back to the library the day before your paper is due to try to find a source again because you forgot to write down the year a book was published, etc. If you record detailed information on your working bibliography while you do your research, writing your list of Works Cited will be a breeze.

The information about doing a list of Works Cited begins on page 241.

Books and Videos

To find **books and videos** on your topic, use the **library catalog.** Go to one of the computers in your library and open the catalog page. Type in the subject that you are researching, and the computer will pull up a list of books and videos on that subject.

Here's what you will see when the computer pulls up the list of books and videos on your subject. The top line is the **title** of the book or video. The second line is the **author's name.** The last line is the **call number** and the **date** when that book or video was published.

The Life of Benjamin Franklin
Lemay, J. A. Leo (Joseph A. Leo), 1935–
E 302.6 .F8 L424   2005

The First Scientific American: Benjamin Franklin and the Pursuit of Genius
Chaplin, Joyce E.
Q 143 .F8 C47   2006

Ben Franklin [video recording]
Herrmann, Edward.
E 302.6 .F8 B453   2004 DVD

Look through the list for any books or videos that might be useful. Write down the **title** and the **call number** for the books or videos you want to find in the library. Now you can go looking for the book or video. Each bookshelf in the library will have a sign telling what call numbers are in that section of shelves.

When you find books or videos that look useful, you can check them out at the checkout desk usually located near the front of the library.

Turn to pages 242 and 267 to see how to list books and videos on your **Working Bibliography.**

Encyclopedias and Other Reference Books

The library has a special section of shelves that contain all kinds of reference books. Reference books are books that you can't check out from the library. You can only use them in the library.

You will find general encyclopedias like *Encyclopedia Britannica, Collier's Encyclopedia,* etc. These encyclopedias have information about a wide range of subjects.

Your library will also have more specific encyclopedias and reference books such as books about history, science, art, etc. These books may have more detailed information than the general encyclopedias.

If you find an article in a reference book that looks useful, the best thing to do is to use one of the copiers in the library to copy the article. You may have to pay a few cents per page to make the copies, but spending a little bit of money will save you a lot of time sitting in the library and copying the article by hand.

Turn to page 250 to see how to list encyclopedias and reference books on your Working Bibliography.

Articles in Magazines, Newspapers, and Journals

To find **articles** about your subject, go to one of the computers in the library and open up the page for the **databases.** To use databases, type in your subject, and the computer will pull up a list of articles on that subject. Click on an article that looks useful, and the computer will pull up that article for you.

Scholarly articles in Journals usually begin with an **abstract.** An abstract is a brief summary of the information in that article. Abstracts can save you time because you can read them quickly to see if the article has the information that you are looking for.

If you find an article that looks useful, you can save it to your USB drive, email it to yourself, or print out a hard copy.

Different libraries subscribe to different databases, and these can sometimes be tricky to navigate, so don't hesitate to ask for help from the library staff if you have any trouble finding what you need.

Turn to page 254 to see how to list articles on your Working Bibliography.

Web Sites

You can search the internet either on the computers at the library or on your own computer at home. Finding information on the internet can be very easy, but you will need to be careful to evaluate each web site and make sure it is accurate and unbiased. See the text box below for guidance with evaluating your sources.

If you find useful information on a web site, you can print a hard copy of the page or copy the information and paste it into a document to save it.

*Turn to page 263 to see how to list internet sources on your **Working Bibliography.***

Evaluating Sources

Accuracy

When you go to the library and find a book on your topic, you can be fairly sure that the information in that book will be accurate and reliable. The library only buys books that are published by reputable publishing companies. A reputable publishing company only publishes books by authors who are experts in their field, and an editor reads the book carefully to check its accuracy. Most newspapers and magazines have a similar process for ensuring that the information they print is accurate.

The internet has a tremendous amount of information, but you will need to evaluate each site to see if it is reliable. Who created the website? Who wrote the article or entry? If you can't tell, or if the site doesn't give the author's credentials, maybe you should look for a different site. Most professors will not accept information found on Wikipedia because anyone can post information to that site. Wikipedia can be a useful research tool, however, because you can find a list of more reliable sources at the bottom of most Wikipedia entries.

Bias

By reading a variety of sources, you will be able to tell if one of the sources is biased. If several sources give similar interpretations of an event, and another source gives a totally different interpretation, consider why this source is so different. Does the author have special knowledge that makes his/her opinion more valid? Or does the author have a personal bias for or against the issue that makes his/her opinion less valid?

Dates

For some research topics, such as climate change, it is important that your information be current. Check the date when the source was written to make sure the information is up-to-date. For other topics, such as Benjamin Franklin, older sources are fine.

Second Skill: Paraphrasing

When you **paraphrase**, you read something, think about what it means, and rewrite the information in your own words. You do not need to include every detail from the original text. Include the information that you believe is important and leave out the rest, but be careful not to change the meaning of the text.

Read the following original text, and then compare it to the paraphrases below.

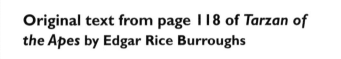

Original text from page 118 of *Tarzan of the Apes* by Edgar Rice Burroughs

From the time Tarzan left the tribe of great anthropoids in which he had been raised, it was torn by continual strife and discord.

Terkoz proved a cruel and capricious king, so that, one by one, many of the older and weaker apes, upon whom he was particularly prone to vent his brutish nature, took their families and sought the quiet and safety of the far interior.

But at last those who remained were driven to desperation by the continued truculence of Terkoz, and it so happened that one of them recalled the parting admonition of

Tarzan: "If you have a chief who is cruel, do not do as the other apes do, and attempt, any one of you, to pit yourself against him alone. But, instead, let two or three or four of you attack him together. Then if you will do this, no chief will dare to be other than he should be, for four of you can kill any chief who may ever be over you."

And the ape who recalled this wise counsel repeated it to several of his fellows, so that when Terkoz returned to the tribe that day he found a warm reception awaiting him.

There were no formalities. As Terkoz reached the group, five huge, hairy beasts sprang upon him. At heart he was an arrant coward, which is the way with bullies among apes as well as among men, so he did not remain to fight and die, but tore himself away from them as quickly as he could and fled into the sheltering boughs of the forest.

Two more attempts he made to rejoin the tribe, but on each occasion he was set upon and driven away. At last he gave it up, and turned, foaming with rage and hatred, into the jungle.

Paraphrase #1

Badly Written: Copying the Words and the Sentence Structure

From the time Tarzan left, the tribe was torn by continual strife. Terkoz was a cruel and capricious king, so many of the older and weaker apes moved to the quiet and safety of another part of the jungle. An ape who remained recalled the advice of Tarzan. Tarzan told them to let two or three or four apes attack a bad king together. So when Terkoz returned to the tribe, five apes sprang upon him. Terkoz was a coward, so he did not fight back, but ran away into the forest. Two more times he tried to return to the tribe, but each time he was attacked and driven away (Burroughs 118).

Paraphrase #2

Badly Written: Changing the Words but Copying the Sentence Structures

From the time Tarzan left, the apes were troubled by constant problems. Terkoz was a mean and evil ruler, so many of the older and feebler apes moved to the peace and stability of another part of the jungle. An ape who remained remembered the advice of Tarzan. Tarzan told them to have several apes jump on a bad ruler together. When Terkoz came back to the tribe, five big, shaggy animals jumped on him. In his heart he was a big baby, so he didn't stay to fight and get killed, but he got away from the apes as fast as he could and ran into the jungle. Two more times he tried to return to the group, but each time he was attacked and chased away (Burroughs 118).

Paraphrase #3

Well Written: Changing the Words and the Sentence Structures

The apes did not get along peacefully after Tarzan left. The new king of the apes, Terkoz, was very harsh and mean. Many of the other apes moved farther into the jungle to get away from him. One of the apes who stayed in the community remembered some advice that Tarzan had given before he left. Tarzan had said that the apes should work together to get rid of a bad king. So five apes attacked Terkoz all at once. Terkoz was afraid, so he ran away into the jungle. He tried to come back twice, but the other apes would not let him return (Burroughs 118).

Guided Instructions for Paraphrasing

Answer the following questions to analyze the three examples of paraphrase on the previous page.

1. Imagine that you are a professor reading Paraphrase #1. Even if you had never read the original text, why might you suspect that the student had not really put this information into his own words?

2. Imagine that you are a professor reading the Paraphrase #3. Even if you had never read the original text, why would you believe that the student had been careful to put all the information into his own words?

> Original texts often have a formal, academic style or tone. When you write a paper, **your writing should sound like you.** How often do most people use the word *capricious*? While it is important to use an appropriate level of formality in a research paper, your writing should be clear and sound natural, not stuffy or artificial.

See page 143 for more info about wordiness and choice of language.

3. Look for places where Paraphrase #1 uses the same words as the original text; this is called plagiarism.

4. How do Paraphrase #2 and Paraphrase #3 change those words?

5. Find some places where Paraphrase #2 and Paraphrase #3 do use the same words as the original text. Why is it necessary to use those exact words?

When you paraphrase, you must **change the words that can be changed**. What are some different ways you could express the idea of *continual strife*? You could say *fighting all the time* or *always arguing* or *didn't get along well*, etc. Since there are several ways you could change the words *continual strife*, those words must be changed or you will be plagiarizing.

Some words in the original text cannot be changed. If the ape king's name is *Terkoz*, you can't call him *Steve* just to use a different word. Since you really can't change that word, you don't have to change it. The same is true for names of places, dates, etc.

6. Compare the first sentence of Paraphrase #2 to the first sentence of the original text. The words in Paraphrase #2 have been changed from the original text, so that's good. But the sentence structures all the way through Paraphrase #2 are very close or identical to the sentence structures of the original text.

7. How does Paraphrase #3 use different sentence structures for the first sentence and all the way through?

In Paraphrase #3 the parts of the sentences are re-arranged so that the paraphrased sentences are quite different from the original text.

If you need to paraphrase information that includes words you can't change, be sure to rearrange the parts of the sentence:

Original text: Benjamin Franklin was born on January 17, 1706, in Boston.

Paraphrase: Benjamin Franklin was born in Boston in 1706.

Writers often include some quotations within their paraphrase. This allows the writer to copy some words from the original that are important in meaning or that express an idea vividly.

Paraphrase #4

Well-Written: Changing the Words and the Sentence Structures but Including Some Quotes:

The apes did not get along peacefully after Tarzan left. The new king of the apes, Terkoz, was "cruel and capricious" (Burroughs 118). Many of the other apes moved farther into the jungle to get away from him. One of the apes who stayed in the community remembered some advice that Tarzan had given them before he left. Tarzan had said that the apes should work together to get rid of a bad king. So five apes attacked Terkoz all at once. Terkoz was "an arrant coward," so he "fled into the sheltering boughs of the forest" (Burroughs 118). He tried to come back twice, but the other apes would not let him return (Burroughs 118).

Instructions for including quotes in your writing begin on page 200.

Instructions for including in-text citations begin on page 216.

Paraphrase vs. Summary

A **summary** is just like a paraphrase except that it is much shorter. Here is an example of a well-written summary of the same original text:

Terkoz, the new king, was mean, so some of the apes left the community. Other apes followed Tarzan's advice and cooperated to drive Terkoz away (Burroughs 118).

Tips for Paraphrasing

1. Work on about half of a paragraph at a time. If you try to work in smaller sections, such as one sentence at a time, paraphrasing will be difficult.

2. Some original texts can be difficult to understand. Read slowly and carefully. Look up unfamiliar words. Think how you could explain the information so that your reader can understand it easily.

3. When the information is clear in your mind, write it down in your own words without looking at the original text. Your version will probably be shorter than the original.

4. Finally, compare your paraphrase to the original text. Make sure that the information is the same but the words and sentence structures are different.

The Two Essentials of Paraphrasing

1. Change the words that can be changed. Don't worry about words that can't be changed (names, places, dates, etc.).

2. Change the sentence structure so that your sentence is really different from the original.

Exercise 10.1 Practice Paraphrasing

Paraphrase this excerpt from page 125 of *Tarzan of the Apes* by Edgar Rice Burroughs. Remember, your paraphrase will probably be shorter than the original text. You can leave out any information that you don't think is important.

Be careful to **change all the words that can be changed** and to **change the sentence structures**.

Original Text from page 125 of *Tarzan of the Apes* by Edgar Rice Burroughs

For several days Terkoz wandered aimlessly, nursing his spite and looking for some weak thing on which to vent his pent anger. It was in this state of mind that the horrible, manlike beast, swinging from tree to tree, came suddenly upon two women in the jungle. He was right above them when he discovered them.

The first intimation Jane Porter had of his presence was when the great hairy body dropped to the earth beside her, and she saw the awful face and the snarling, hideous mouth thrust within a foot of her. One piercing scream escaped her lips as the brute hand clutched her arm. Then she was dragged toward those awful fangs which yawned at her throat. But ere they touched her throat, another mood claimed the anthropoid.

The tribe had kept his women. He must find others to replace them. This hairless white ape would be the first of his new household, and so he threw her roughly across his broad, hairy shoulders and leaped back into the trees, bearing Jane away while Esmeralda screamed with terror.

> The sudden advent of the ape had confused Jane to such an extent that she thought now that he was bearing her toward the beach. For this reason she conserved her energies and her voice until she could see that they had approached near enough to the camp to attract the succor she craved.
>
> She could not have known it, but she was being borne farther and farther into the impenetrable jungle.

Third Skill: Quotations

Most professors will expect you to include some quotations in a research essay. Quotations add variety to your writing and credibility to your argument. First we will learn how to use quotes effectively, and then we will learn how to punctuate quotes correctly.

Guided Instructions for Quotations:

Look back at the essay about Benjamin Franklin on pages 175–181. Answer these questions to analyze Tiffany's use of quotations in her essay.

1. How many quotations did Tiffany use in her essay?

2. How does the number of quotations relate to the number of paragraphs in the essay?

There is no strict rule about how many quotations should be in a research essay.

Some paragraphs may not have any quotations, and other paragraphs may have two or more. You want to have a good balance between the number of quotations and the length of your essay. **About one or two quotations per paragraph is a good guideline**, but this is not a rule that you need to follow strictly.

3. How long are the quotations?

Most of your quotations should be short. Your paper should be mostly your own words (paraphrase). If you want to use a longer quotation—four or more lines of typing—set it off as a **block quote** by indenting the entire quotation ten spaces. The indentation shows the reader that this is a quotation, so you don't need to use quotation marks. Look at paragraph 6 in the sample essay about Franklin to see an example of a block quote.

4. Why did the author choose to quote these passages in her essay?

The author copied words from her sources that she thought were **important in meaning or wording**. She could have put the information into her own words if she wanted to, but she decided that using the exact words from a source would sound more powerful.

5. Is each quotation smoothly integrated into the sentence?

> Yes, **the author's own words flow smoothly into each quotation.** Compare the two sentences below, and explain why the first sentence is smooth and the second sentence is not smooth:
>
> > Franklin had "an infectious sense of wonder and curiosity" for a wide variety of topics.
> >
> > Franklin was interested in a wide variety of topics "an infectious sense of wonder and curiosity."

6. Where did the author put information from her sources into her own words rather than copying the source and using quotation marks?

> **Most of the information in this essay is in the author's own words.** This is called *paraphrasing.*

Turn to page 190 for an explanation of paraphrasing.

7. Which quotations include an ellipsis? An ellipsis is three periods with spaces in between them.

> The quotations in paragraphs 3, 6, and 8 have an **ellipsis** to show that the author left out some of the words from the original text.

8. Find several places where the author obviously left some words off of the quotation but did NOT use an ellipsis. Why didn't the author use an ellipsis on those quotations?

You must use an ellipsis to show the reader that you left off some words **only when the reader wouldn't otherwise know it.** If your quotation is not a complete sentence, it's obvious that you must have left off words, so you don't need to use ellipses.

> He held "rock star status in Europe and some quarters of the United States."

If you leave some words out but your quotation is still a complete sentence, put an ellipsis where you left off the words, at the beginning of the quotation, in the middle, and/or at the end. Of course, be sure that you don't change the meaning of the quotation when you leave off words.

9. Where did the author use square brackets [ ] in a quotation?

> In paragraph 3, the author wanted to explain the meaning of the words *prudence* and *industry*. **Any time you need to insert your own words into a quotation, put square brackets around the words you are inserting: [wisdom] [hard work].**

> What if the source you are quoting from has a mistake, like a misspelling? When you are quoting, you must copy the original source exactly. You can use the Latin word *sic,* which means *thus,* to tell the reader that this mistake was in the original source and you just copied it: "He was a man of great viger [sic] and energy."

Three Essentials of Quoting

1. Don't use too many quotes. Most of your paper should be in your own words (paraphrasing and summarizing). Most of your quotes should be short.

2. Be selective about the words you choose to quote. Quote words that are important in meaning or wording. Don't worry about putting quotation marks around words you can't change (names, places, dates, etc.).

3. Be sure that your own words and the quoted words flow smoothly together.

Punctuating Quotations

Rules for Punctuating Quotations:

1. Be careful to **copy the words and punctuation exactly.**

2. Be careful to **put quotation marks around only the words you copied.**

3. If the original text has quotation marks in it already, put regular double quote marks around the entire quotation and **turn the original's quote marks into single quotation marks.** Don't worry if this gives you three quote marks in a row either at the beginning or the end of the quote:

Original Text: The maxim of the British people is "Business as usual."

Correct Quotation: "The maxim of the British people is 'Business as usual.'"

4. Use an **ellipsis** (three periods with spaces in between) to show where you left some words out of a quote ONLY when the reader would not otherwise know that words were left out.

His final argument is " … they are so grateful!!"

5. Use **square brackets** [ ] around words that you insert into a quote.

He used the pen name Richard Saunders and wrote articles "praising prudence [wisdom], industry [hard work], and honesty."

6. Be careful where you put the period at the end of a quote. If an in-text citation comes right after a quote, **save the period for after the in-text citation.** If you don't have an in-text citation right after the quote, **put the period inside the quotation marks:**

Franklin believed that his experiments and inventions "could advance the course of scientific and philosophical knowledge" (Dillon).

According to Dillon, Franklin believed that his experiments and inventions "could advance the course of scientific and philosophical knowledge."

7. **A long quote** (more than four lines of typing) should be set off as a **block quote**. Block quotes are punctuated differently in two ways:

1) Instead of using quotation marks, **indent the quote ten spaces** from the left margin.

2) Put the **period that ends the quote before the in-text citation.**

… I cannot help expressing a wish, that every member of the convention, who may still have objections to it, would with me on this occasion doubt a little of his own infallibility, and to make manifest our unanimity, put his name to this instrument. (qtd. in Isaacson 364–65)

Exercise 10.2 Punctuating Quotations

Look at each incorrect quotation and try to find the mistakes. Then rewrite the quotation with correct punctuation. Compare your work to the correctly punctuated quotations on page 208.

1. Original Text by Benjamin Franklin:

Keep your eyes wide open before marriage, half shut afterwards.

Quotation with Incorrect Punctuation:

Keep your eyes "wide open" before marriage, but keep them "half shut" afterwards.

Your Version:

2. Original Text by Will Rogers:

I never met a man I didn't like.

Quotation with Incorrect Punctuation:

Will Rogers said, "he never met a man he didn't like".

Your Version:

3. Original Text by Joan Didion:

O'Keefe is neither crusty nor eccentric. She is simply hard, a straight shooter, a woman clean of received wisdom and open to what she sees.

Quotation with Incorrect Punctuation:

"O'Keefe is neither crusty nor eccentric." "She is simply hard, a straight shooter, a woman clean of received wisdom and open to what she sees."

Your Version:

4. Original Text by Benjamin Franklin:

There are three faithful friends—an old wife, an old dog, and ready money.

Quotation with Incorrect Punctuation:

"There are three faithful friends says Franklin—an old wife, an old dog, and ready money."

Your Version:

5. Original Text by Ralph Waldo Emerson:

The ancient precept "Know Thyself" and the modern precept "Study Nature" become at last one maxim.

Quotation with Incorrect Punctuation:

"The ancient precept "Know Thyself " and the modern precept "Study Nature" become at last one maxim".

Your Version:

Answers and Explanations:

1. "Keep your eyes wide open before marriage," but keep them "half shut afterwards."

Explanation: Be very precise about putting quotation marks around the words copied from the original.

2. Will Rogers said, "I never met a man I didn't like."

Explanation: When you quote, copy all the words exactly. Put the period inside the closing quotation mark.

3. "O'Keefe is neither crusty nor eccentric. She is simply hard, a straight shooter, a woman clean of received wisdom and open to what she sees."

Explanation: When your quote is two or more sentences long, you don't need to put quotation marks at the end of one sentence and the beginning of the next sentence. Just keep going until the end of the quoted material.

4. "There are three faithful friends" says Franklin, "—an old wife, an old dog, and ready money."

Explanation: Be careful that you don't put any of your own words within the quotation marks. *Says Franklin* should not be inside the quotation marks.

5. "The ancient precept 'Know Thyself' and the modern precept 'Study Nature' become at last one maxim."

Explanation: Use single quotation marks to show the words that were in quotation marks in the original. Put the period inside the closing quotation mark.

Putting Paraphrase and Quotation Together

Now that you have learned how to paraphrase and how to do quotations, you can put both skills together. Most professors will want you to include some quotations in your research paper, so develop the skill of selecting effective quotations, incorporating them into your paraphrase, and punctuating everything correctly.

Exercise 10.3 Including Quotations in Your Paraphrase

Paraphrase this excerpt from *Tarzan of the Apes* by Edgar Rice Burroughs. Remember, your paraphrase will probably be shorter than the original text. You can leave out any information that you don't think is important.

Be careful to **change all the words that can be changed** and to **change the sentence structures.**

Choose **one or two quotations** to include in your paraphrase. Select **short quotations** that are **important in meaning or wording.** Make sure that your own words and the quoted words flow smoothly together.

Original Text from page 132 of *Tarzan of the Apes* by Edgar Rice Burroughs

Tarzan quickly gathered up fruit, and, bringing it, laid it at Jane's feet; and then he sat upon the drum beside her, and with his knife opened and prepared the various fruits for her meal. Together and in silence they ate, occasionally stealing sly glances at one another, until finally Jane broke into a merry laugh in which Tarzan joined.

"I wish you spoke English," said the girl.

Tarzan shook his head, and an expression of wistful and pathetic longing sobered his laughing eyes.

Again he rose and went into the trees, but first he tried to explain by means of signs that he would return shortly, and he did so well that Jane understood and was not afraid when he had gone. Shortly he returned from the jungle and in a few minutes reappeared with a quantity of soft grasses and ferns. Two more trips he made until he had quite a pile of material at hand.

Then he spread the ferns and grasses upon the ground in a soft, flat bed, and above it leaned many branches together so that they met a few feet over its center. Upon these he spread layers of huge leaves of the great elephant's ear, and with more branches and more leaves he closed one end of the little shelter he had built.

It was growing dark now, and so they ate again of the fruit which was both food and drink for them; then Tarzan rose, and leading Jane to the little bower he had erected, motioned her to go within.

For the first time in hours, a feeling of fear swept over her, and Tarzan felt her draw away as though shrinking from him.

So Tarzan of the Apes did the only thing he knew to assure Jane of her safety. He removed his hunting knife from its sheath and handed it to her hilt first, again motioning her into the bower.

Jane understood, and taking the long knife she entered and lay down upon the soft grasses while Tarzan of the apes stretched himself upon the ground across the entrance.

And thus the rising sun found them in the morning.

Fourth Skill: Taking Notes

Taking notes is probably the most time-consuming step of writing a research paper. Follow these guidelines when you take notes, and you will save yourself a lot of time.

1. You can write your notes on **index cards** or **notebook paper,** or you can type them directly onto the **computer.** If you use notebook paper, **write only on one side of the paper.** This way, when it's time to rearrange your information, you can cut apart your notes without losing the information on the back side.

2. Each note should be **short.** If you write on index cards, each note will have to be short because you will run out of space on the card. If you write on notebook paper or type on the computer, write a little bit and then **leave several blank lines** on the page before writing the next note.

3. Write **a key word** at the top of each note. The key word shows you at a glance what type of information is covered in that note. This will be helpful when it's time to rearrange your notes to create paragraphs in your paper. When Tiffany took notes on Franklin, her key words included terms like *childhood, writing, inventions,* and *politics.*

4. Write an **in-text citation** at the end of each note. This citation will tell your reader where that information came from. Writing all those citations may seem repetitive when you have a page of notes and each note has the same citation at its end. But including a citation after each note allows you to rearrange the notes later without losing track of which source each note came from. When your paper is nearly finished, it is not fun to have to go through one of your sources again trying to find a bit of information because you forgot to write down the page number when you were taking notes.

We will learn how to do in-text citations beginning on page 225.

5. Be careful about **paraphrasing** and **quoting**. If you paraphrase, be sure to put the information completely in your own words. If you copy word-for-word directly from the source, write quotation marks around the words you copied so you remember that those words came from the source.

Example of a page of notes written on notebook paper:

Childhood

When he was 12 he to work for his brother James in a print shop. Ben loved the print shop even though James was mean to him. Ben was a good writer, but James wouldn't publish his work. So Ben wrote things under the pen name Mrs. Silence Dogood, and James printed the articles, and readers loved them. When James found out Ben had really written them, he was very mad. ("Benjamin")

Childhood

Ben quit working at the print shop and ran away to New York where he lived for a little while but then he went to Philadelphia, which was "his home base for the rest of his life." ("Benjamin")

Writing

He bought The Pennsylvania Gazette newspaper. Wrote Poor Richard's Almanack in 1732 ("Benjamin")

Marriage

Married Deborah Read in 1730. ("Benjamin")

Public Service

Started the first fire Company "to counteract dangerous fire hazards," started a free public library "so others could share his passion for reading" and was appointed postmaster for Philadelphia. ("Benjamin")

Things to Notice

- Each note is short.

- Each note starts with a key word.

- Words copied directly from the source are in quotation marks.

- Each note ends with an in-text citation.

- There are blank lines in between all the notes.

Fifth Skill: Documenting Sources with In-Text Citations and Signal Phrases

When you write a research paper, you must tell your reader the source for each bit of information. Some documentation styles do this with footnotes or endnotes. The **MLA documentation style uses in-text citations** (parentheses) **and signal phrases.**

Documenting your sources with in-text citations and signal phrases can seem confusing, but really it is quite logical. First we will learn how to use in-text citations, and then we will learn how to use signal phrases.

Using In-Text Citations

The purpose of in-text citations is to show your reader which source each bit of information came from. The in-text citation goes at the end of a quote or a section of paraphrased information.

This version of Tiffany's paper uses only in-text citations, no signal phrases. Do the following two exercises to analyze the in-text citations in this version of the essay on Franklin, and you will see how they work to show the reader which source each bit of information came from.

Tiffany Bradshaw

Professor Anders

English 111

16 April 2017

America's Renaissance Man

Most United States money displays the face of a former president: George Washington appears on the dollar bill and the quarter; Abraham Lincoln is on the five dollar bill and the penny; Thomas Jefferson is on the nickel, and Franklin Delano Roosevelt is on the dime. But the hundred dollar bill has the face of Benjamin Franklin, a man who never held any public office. What earned Franklin his place on the hundred dollar bill? Benjamin Franklin is "best remembered for his role in separating the American colonies from Great Britain," but politics was only one of his many interests ("Franklin"). Franklin had "an infectious sense of wonder and curiosity" for a wide variety of topics (Dillon). An examination of Franklin's remarkable life shows that it was his successful leadership in many different areas that made him an important figure in American history.

Bradshaw 2

Benjamin Franklin was born in Boston, Massachusetts, in 1706; his father was a tradesman who made soap and candles. When Franklin was ten years old, his father took him out of school to help in the family business. Franklin found this work boring, however, so at the age of twelve, he began an apprenticeship in the printing shop of his older brother, James. Franklin became interested in writing, but James refused to publish his work, so Franklin sent articles to James under the pen name Mrs. Silence Dogood. Readers loved these articles, but when James found out that they had really been written by his brother, James became very angry. So Franklin left the print shop in Boston and eventually moved to Philadelphia ("Benjamin").

Franklin worked at several different jobs in Philadelphia including bookkeeping, shop keeping, and printing. Finally, in 1728, he and a partner started their own print shop. ("Benjamin"). Around 1729 he began publishing a newspaper called the *Pennsylvania Gazette,* and in 1732 he started a series of magazines called *Poor Richard's Almanac.* He used the pen name Richard Saunders and wrote articles "praising prudence [wisdom], industry [hard work], and honesty" ("Franklin"). These articles use a humorous tone to offer common-sense advice to readers. In one article titled "Reasons to Choose an Older Mistress," Franklin describes eight reasons why it is better to date an older woman than a young woman. His final argument is " … they are so grateful!!" (qtd. in Isaacson 125). Not quite following his own advice, Franklin married a young woman named Deborah Read. They were married for forty-four years and had three children ("Benjamin").

In 1748 Franklin stopped working at the newspaper and focused on science ("Franklin"). Franklin believed that his experiments and inventions "could advance the course of scientific and philosophical knowledge" (Dillon). Some of Franklin's many inventions include bifocal glasses, the glass harmonica, and the free-standing wood stove. His famous experiment of flying a kite in a thunderstorm helped him understand electricity, and this led to his invention of the lightning rod and a battery for storing electricity (Dillon). Franklin was now a leading citizen of Philadelphia, and he used his position to start several projects for the benefit of others. He started the first fire department, a free lending library, and a school that later became the University of Pennsylvania ("Franklin").

Between 1757 and 1775, Franklin was selected to represent the interests of Pennsylvania and several other colonies in England, so he spent several years living in London working to promote the colonies' interests with the English government. In 1775, seeing that there could soon be a war between England and the colonies, Franklin returned home ("Franklin"). Franklin played an important role in the fight for independence and the development of a new government for the young United States of America. He served as a delegate to the Second Continental Congress, was one of the five men who wrote the Declaration of Independence, and was one of the thirteen who wrote the Articles of Confederation ("Benjamin"). At the beginning of the Revolutionary War, Franklin travelled to France to ask the French government to help the colonies by providing money and military assistance ("Franklin"). In 1783, after the Revolutionary War ended, Franklin and several other diplomats negotiated the peace treaty with England ("Benjamin").

In 1785 Franklin served as Pennsylvania's representative to the Constitutional Convention where he played an important role in writing the Constitution and electing George Washington as the first president ("Benjamin"). Writing the Constitution was a difficult task, and the members had different opinions about how the new government should be set up. Anger and arguing began to replace calm discussion. After months of work and debate, some of the representatives still did not want to sign the new Constitution. Franklin's wisdom and humility can be seen in this excerpt of the closing speech he made to the members of the Constitutional Convention.

> I confess that I do not entirely approve this Constitution at present, but sir, I am not sure I shall never approve it: for having lived long, I have experienced many instances of being obliged, by better information or fuller consideration, to change opinions even on important subjects, which I once thought right, but found to be otherwise. It is therefore that the older I grow the more apt I am to doubt my own judg-ment, and to pay more respect to the judgment of others.... I cannot help ex-pressing a wish, that every member of the convention, who may still have objections to it, would with me on this occasion doubt a little of his own infallibility, and to make manifest our unanimity, put his name to this instrument. (qtd. in Isaacson 364–65)

Bradshaw 5

After the adoption of the Constitution, Franklin continued to work for the betterment of society. He worked to end slavery by serving as president for the Pennsylvania Society for Promoting the Abolition of Slavery ("Benjamin").

In his later years, Franklin received many honors. He held "rock star status in Europe and some quarters of the United States" (Dillon). In France, his supporters hired a famous sculptor to make a statue of Franklin. The inscription at the bottom of the statue reads, "He snatched the lightning from the sky and the scepter [royal staff] from tyrants" (Dillon). He was awarded honorary degrees from several prestigious universities including Harvard, Yale, Oxford, and the University of England. Benjamin Franklin died in 1790 at the age of eighty-four after suffering from gout and other illnesses for several years ("Benjamin").

Franklin became an essential figure in American history through his writing, his inventions, his diplomacy, his public service, and his wisdom in working with others to create a new government. His example clearly inspired other Americans, for "when Davy Crocket died at the Alamo in 1836, almost fifty years after Franklin's death, the book he had in his pocket was not the Bible, but a copy of Franklin's *Autobiography*" (Dillon). He was "a man who never finished school but shaped his life through abundant reading and experience, a strong moral compass and an unflagging commitment to civic duty, and an overall wit, good humor and integrity" ("Benjamin"). Clearly, Franklin deserves his place on the hundred dollar bill.

Works Cited

"Benjamin Franklin Biography." *Bio*. A&E Television Networks, 17 Nov. 2015. www.biography.com/people/benjamin-franklin-9301234.

Dillon, James J. "Benjamin Franklin: A Wonder-Based Approach to Life and Learning." *Encounter*, vol. 22 no. 4, 2009, pp. 38-47. Ebsco Host, www.connection.ebscohost.com/c/articles/49007048/benjamin-franklin-wonder-based-approach-life-learning.

"Franklin, Benjamin." *Encyclopedia Britanica*. 1998.

Isaccson, Walter. *A Benjamin Franklin Reader*. Simon and Schuster, 2003.

Exercise 10.4 Color-Coding of Sources in an Essay with In-Text Citations

Use colored pencils, markers, or high-lighters in four different colors to analyze the in-text citations used in the essay on Benjamin Franklin which begins on page 217.

Step 1. Use your first color to highlight the first source listed on the list of Works Cited: the website article titled "Benjamin Franklin."

Step 2. Use that same color to highlight every citation that has the name "Benjamin."

Step 3. Starting with each citation you have colored for "Benjamin," work backwards and color in the text of the essay until you come to the beginning of the paragraph or a citation with a different name in it.

Now everything in this essay that came from the website article titled "Benjamin Franklin" is highlighted with your first color.

Step 4. Use your second color to highlight the second source listed on the list of Works Cited: the article by James Dillon.

Step 5. Use that same color to highlight every citation that has the name Dillon.

Step 6. Starting with each citation you have colored for Dillon, work backwards and color in the text of the essay until you come to the beginning of a paragraph or a citation with a different name in it.

Now everything in this essay that came from the article by James Dillon is highlighted with your second color.

Step 7. Use your third color to highlight the third source listed on the list of Works Cited: the encyclopedia article titled "Franklin, Benjamin."

Step 8. Use that same color to highlight every citation that has the name "Franklin."

Step 9. Starting with each citation you have colored for "Franklin," work backwards and color in the text of the essay until you come to the beginning of a paragraph or a citation with a different name in it.

Now everything in this essay that came from the encyclopedia article is highlighted with your third color.

Step 10. Use your fourth color to highlight the fourth source listed on the list of Works Cited: the book edited by Walter Isaacson.

Step 11. Use that same color to highlight every citation that includes the name Isaacson.

Step 12. Starting with each citation you have colored for Isaacson, work backwards and color in the text of the essay until you come to the beginning of a paragraph or a citation with a different name in it.

Now everything in this essay that came from the book edited by Isaacson is highlighted with your fourth color.

Look at the highlighted essay and notice that nearly everything is highlighted one of your four colors.

Only the thesis statement (last sentence of the first paragraph) and the very last sentence are not highlighted. These sentences are the author's own thoughts and opinions. As you can see, the in-text citations show the reader which information came from each source on the list of Works Cited.

Exercise 10.5 Guided Analysis of In-Text Citations

Analyze the use of in-text citations in the essay you just highlighted.

1. Where has the student put in-text citations in her essay?

> The student put a citation **at the end of every sentence that includes a quotation.** She also put a citation **at the end of each section of paraphrased information.** By looking at your highlighted colors, you can see that a citation marks the end of a section of paraphrased information.

2. Find a place where a section of one color is only one sentence long.

> Sometimes the sections are quite short because Tiffany switched between her sources frequently.

3. What is the longest section of one color in the essay?

The information in paragraph two all came from the web article titled "Benjamin Franklin." Since there are no quotations in this paragraph, only one citation is needed.

4. Can you find a place where the citation comes in the middle of the sentence?

No. **Save the citation for the end of the sentence.** The only time you would put a citation in the middle of a sentence would be if the first part of the sentence came from one source and the second part came from another source:

People in France hired a sculptor to make a statue of Franklin (Dillon), and several universities awarded him honorary degrees ("Benjamin").

5. Does the period go before or after the citation?

Notice that **the period which ends the sentence comes after the citation** except in the block quotation where it comes before the citation.

6. Can you find a citation that contains more than just one word?

In paragraphs 3 and 6 we see something unusual: (qtd. in Isaacson). The quotation is Franklin's own words, not Isaacson's words. Since Tiffany read Franklin's words in the book edited by Isaacson, she has cited the quotation to Isaacson.

7. Do any of the citations in this essay include page numbers?

Only the citations for the book edited by Isaacson contain page numbers. Tiffany did not need to use page numbers for her other sources. The two sources she got from the internet didn't have page numbers, and *Encyclopedia Britanica* is a reference book that is arranged alphabetically. If someone wants to look up Benjamin Franklin in an alphabetical reference book such as an encyclopedia, he or she would turn to the F section and never even look at the page numbers.

You should **include the page numbers for sources such as books, magazines, or newspapers that have page numbers.** Look carefully at the citation for Isaacson, and you will see that only one blank space comes between the name Isaacson and the page number. You don't need to use a comma or type *pg.* or *page.*

Page numbers from newspaper articles are usually a letter for the section of the newspaper and then a number for the page in that section.

See page 258 for more information about page numbers for news- paper articles.

Five Essentials of In-Text Citations

1. Put an in-text citation at the end of every sentence that includes a quotation.

2. For paraphrased or summarized informa- tion, put an in-text citation when you are fin- ished with information from one source and

you are about start on information from another source.

3. The word in the citation is the first word of
the Works Cited listing for that source. Usually
the first word will be the author's last name. If
the author is unknown, use a shortened version
of the title. Be sure to use quotation marks or
italics to show that these words are a title. You
can see examples of this in Tiffany's essay:
("Franklin") and ("Benjamin").

4. Include the page number for sources that
have page numbers. Just leave one blank space
between the word and the page number; you
don't need to type a comma or *pg.* or *page*.

5. Put the period after the citation *except for
block quotes* for which you put the period before the citation.

Using Signal Phrases

Now that you understand how in-text citations work, we can
learn how to use **signal phrases**.

A signal phrases serves the same purpose as an in-text citation:
it tells the reader which source each bit of information came
from. While an in-text citation goes at the end of a quotation

or section of paraphrase, a signal phrase is usually placed right **before** the quotation or section of paraphrase.

The signal phrase gives the **author's name** and any other information that would help **provide a context for the quote or give credibility to the source.**

Some professors prefer that you introduce every quote or section of paraphrase with a signal phrase; for other professors, you don't have to use signal phrases unless you want to. If you're unsure about using signal phrases, ask your professor for guidance.

Here are some examples of different ways of writing signal phrases. Notice that, when the signal phrase includes a verb, the **verb** in each signal phrase is in the **present tense:**

> According to Dillon, Franklin had "an infectious sense of wonder and curiosity" for a wide variety of topics.

> Noted Franklin biographer James Dillon points out that the French admired him so much that they hired a famous sculptor to create a statue of Franklin.

Since both of these examples are from a website article that doesn't have any page numbers, no in-text citation is needed for these sentences.

Keep reading for more information about when to use an in-text citation along with the signal phrase.

> **Present Tense Verbs Commonly Used in Signal Phrases**
>
> | | | | |
> |---|---|---|---|
> | Argues | Calls | Points out | Believes |
> | Claims | Reports | Thinks | Writes |
> | Denies | Adds | Comments | Admits |
> | Suggests | Declares | Insists | |

Sometimes You Need BOTH an In-Text Citation and a Signal Phrase.

Use an In-Text Citation with a Signal Phrase for Sources That Have Page Numbers.

None of the examples above need an in-text citation because none of these sources has page numbers. If you are quoting or paraphrasing from a source that does have page numbers (such as a book), you will need an in-text citation at the end of that information even though you started with a signal phrase:

> Isaacson notes that Franklin used "gossip, sex, crime, and humor" to boost sales of his newspaper (3).

Use an In-Text Citation with a Signal Phrase When Needed for Clarity.

When you use signal phrases in your writing, make sure that your reader will understand what information came from which source. Read this excerpt and think why the reader might be unclear about where one source ends and the next begins:

Confusing:

According to Dillon, Franklin was so admired in France that his supporters hired a famous sculptor to make a statue of him. He was awarded honorary degrees from several prestigious universities including Harvard, Yale, Oxford, and the University of England. Benjamin Franklin died in 1790 at the age of eighty-four after having suffered from gout and other illnesses for several years ("Benjamin").

We can tell that the first sentence came from Dillon and the last sentence came from "Benjamin," but what about the middle sentence? Did it come from Dillon or "Benjamin"?

To fix this problem, add an in-text citation at the end of the information from Dillon even though his name was given in the signal phrase.

Clear:

According to Dillon, Franklin was so admired in France that his supporters hired a famous sculptor to make a statue of him (Dillon). He was awarded honorary degrees from several prestigious universities including Harvard, Yale, Oxford, and the University of England. Benjamin Franklin died in 1790 at the age of eighty-four after having suffered from gout and other illnesses for several years ("Benjamin").

Exercise 10.6 Writing In-Text Citations and Signal Phrases

For each Works Cited listing, write an in-text citation and a signal phrase. For the in-text citation, use the first word of the Works Cited listing. For the signal phrase, if you don't know the author's name, use the word that you think would work best. For sources that have page numbers, put a page number in the in-text citation. Check your answers on page ____.

EXAMPLES:

"Franklin, Benjamin." *Encyclopedia Britannica.* 1998.

In-Text Citation: ("Franklin")

Signal Phrase: *Britannica* points out that

Isaacson, Walter. *A Benjamin Franklin Reader.* Simon and Schuster, 2003.

In-Text Citation: (Isaacson 53)

Signal Phrase: Isaacson argues that

1. Ehrenreich, Barbara. *Bait and Switch: The (Futile) Pursuit of the American Dream.* Metropolitan, 2005.

   In-Text Citation:

   Signal Phrase:

2. Hamilton, Edith. *Mythology.* Little, Brown, 1942.

   In-Text Citation:

   Signal Phrase:

3. "Colombus, Christopher." *The Columbia Encyclopedia,*
   5th ed., Columbia UP, 1993.
   In-Text Citation:
   Signal Phrase:

4. Edmonds, Patricia. "A Sleighful of Santas, Surveyed."
   National Geographic, Dec. 2016, p. 17.
   In-Text Citation:
   Signal Phrase:

5. "Radioactivity in Drinking Water." *Mother Earth News,*
   Jan. 2017, p. 8.
   In-Text Citation:
   Signal Phrase:

6. "Why Animal Rights?" *PETA,* 2016, www.peta.org/
   why-animal-rights/.
   In-Text Citation:
   Signal Phrase:

7. "John Lee Hooker." *Bio.,* A & E Television Networks,
   2012, www.biography.com/people/john-lee-
   hooker-9343203.
   In-Text Citation:
   Signal Phrase:

Practical Grammar

The following version of the essay on Franklin uses a combination of in-text citations and signal phrases. Do Exercise 10.6 to analyze how the in-text citations and signal phrases work together to show the reader which source each bit of information came from.

Bradshaw 1

Tiffany Bradshaw

Professor Anders

English 111

16 April 2017

America's Renaissance Man

Most United States money displays the face of a former president: George Washington appears on the dollar bill and the quarter; Abraham Lincoln is on the five dollar bill and the penny; Thomas Jefferson is on the nickel, and Franklin Delano Roosevelt is on the dime. But the hundred dollar bill has the face of Benjamin Franklin, a man who never held any public office. What earned Franklin his place on the hundred dollar bill? *Encyclopedia Britanica* argues that, although Benjamin Franklin is "best remembered for his role in separating the American colonies from Great Britain," politics was only one of his many interests. Noted biographer James Dillon writes that Franklin had "an infectious sense of wonder and curiosity" for a wide variety of topics. An examination of Franklin's remarkable life shows that it was his successful leadership in many different areas that made him an important figure in American history.

Benjamin Franklin was born in Boston, Massachusetts, in 1706; his father was a tradesman who made soap and candles. When Franklin was ten years old, his father took him out of school to help with the family business. Franklin found this work boring, however, so at the age of twelve, he began an apprenticeship in the printing shop of his older brother, James. Franklin became interested in writing, but James refused to publish his little brother's work, so Franklin sent articles to James under the pen name Mrs. Silence Dogood. Readers loved the articles, but when James found out that they had really been written by his brother, James became very angry. Consequently, Franklin left the print shop in Boston and eventually moved to Philadelphia ("Benjamin").

According to *Bio*, Franklin worked at several different jobs in Philadelphia including bookkeeping, shop keeping, and printing. Finally, in 1728, he and a partner started their own print shop ("Benjamin"). Around 1729 he began publishing a newspaper called the *Pennsylvania Gazette*, and in 1732 he started a series of magazines called *Poor Richard's Almanac*. He used the pen name Richard Saunders and wrote articles "praising prudence [wisdom], industry [hard work], and honesty" ("Franklin"). These articles use a humorous tone to offer common-sense advice to readers. In one article titled "Reasons to Choose an Older Mistress," Franklin describes eight reasons why it is better to date an older woman than a young woman. His final argument is " … they are so grateful!!" (qtd. in Isaacson 125). *Bio* points out that Franklin did not follow his own advice, however, for he married a young woman named Deborah Read. They were married for forty-four years and had three children.

In 1748 Franklin stopped working at the newspaper and focused on science ("Franklin"). Dillon writes that Franklin believed his experiments and inventions "could advance the course of scientific and philosophical knowledge." Some of Franklin's many inventions include bifocal glasses, the glass harmonica, and the free-standing wood stove. His famous experiment of flying a kite in a thunderstorm helped him understand electricity, and this led to his invention of the lightning rod and a battery for storing electricity (Dillon). Franklin was now a leading citizen of Philadelphia, and he used his position to start several projects for the benefit of others. He started the first fire department, a free lending library, and a school that later became the University of Pennsylvania ("Franklin").

Britanica details Franklin's work as a diplomat between 1757 and 1775. Franklin was selected to represent the interests of Pennsylvania and several other colonies in England, so he spent several years living in London working to promote the colonies' interests with the English government. In 1775, seeing that there could soon be a war between England and the colonies, Franklin returned home. *Bio* describes how Franklin played an important role in the fight for independence and the development of a new government for the young United States of America. He served as a delegate to the Second Continental Congress, was one of the five men who wrote the Declaration of Independence, and was one of the thirteen who wrote the Articles of Confederation ("Benjamin"). At the beginning of the Revolutionary War, Franklin travelled to France to ask the French government to help the colonies by providing money and military assistance ("Franklin"). In 1783, after the Rev-

olutionary War ended, Franklin and several other diplomats negotiated the peace treaty with England ("Benjamin").

According to *Bio*, in 1785 Franklin served as Pennsylvania's representative to the Constitutional Convention where he played an
im-portant role in writing the Constitution and electing George
Washington as the first president. Isaacson suggests that writing the
Constitution was a difficult task, and the members had different
opinions about how the new government should be set up. Anger
and arguing began to replace calm discussion. After months of
work and debate, some of the representatives still did not want to
sign the new Constitution. Franklin's wisdom and humility can be
seen in this excerpt of the closing speech he made to the members
of the Constitutional Convention.

> I confess that I do not entirely approve this Constitution at
> present, but sir, I am not sure I shall never approve it: for
> having lived long, I have experienced many instances of be-
> ing obliged, by better information or fuller consideration, to
> change opinions even on important subjects, which I once
> thought right, but found to be otherwise. It is therefore that
> the older I grow the more apt I am to doubt my own judg-
> ment, and to pay more respect to the judgment of others.... I
> cannot help expressing a wish, that every member of the con-
> vention, who may still have objections to it, would with me
> on this occasion doubt a little of his own infallibility, and to
> make manifest our unanimity, put his name to this instru-
> ment. (qtd. in Isaacson 364–65)

After the adoption of the Constitution, Franklin continued to work for the betterment of society. He worked to end slavery by serving as president for the Pennsylvania Society for Promoting the Abolition of Slavery ("Benjamin").

In his later years, Franklin received many honors. Dillon describes Franklin as achieving "rock star status in Europe and some quarters of the United States." In France, Franklin was so highly re-garded that his supporters hired a famous sculptor to make a statue of him. The inscription at the bottom of the statue reads, "He snatched the lightning from the sky and the scepter [royal staff] from tyrants" (Dillon). Franklin was awarded honorary degrees from several prestigious universities including Harvard, Yale, Oxford, and the University of England. He died in 1790 at the age of eighty-four after suffering from gout and other illnesses for several years ("Benjamin").

Franklin became an essential figure in American history through his writing, his inventions, his diplomacy, his public service, and his wisdom in working with others to create a new government. Dillon points out that Franklin's example clearly inspired other Americans, for "when Davy Crocket died at the Alamo in 1836, almost fifty years after Franklin's death, the book he had in his pocket was not the Bible, but a copy of Franklin's *Autobiography*." *Bio* describes Franklin as "a man who never finished school but shaped his life through abundant reading and experience, a strong moral compass and an unflagging commitment to civic duty, and an overall wit, good humor and integrity." Clearly, Franklin deserves his place on the hundred dollar bill.

Works Cited

"Benjamin Franklin Biography." *Bio.* A&E Television Networks, 17
Nov. 2015. www.biography.com/people/benjamin-franklin-
9301234.

Dillon, James J. "Benjamin Franklin: A Wonder-Based Approach to
Life and Learning." *Encounter*, vol. 22 no. 4, 2009, pp. 38-47.
Ebsco Host, www.connection.ebscohost.com/c/articles/49007048/
benjamin-franklin-wonder-based-approach-life-learning.

"Franklin, Benjamin." *Encyclopedia Britanica.* 1998.

Isaccson, Walter. *A Benjamin Franklin Reader.* Simon and Schuster,
2003.

Exercise 10.7 Color-Coding of Sources in an Essay with In-Text Citations and Signal Phrases

Use colored pencils, markers, or high-lighters in four different colors to analyze the in-text citations and signal phrases used in the essay about Franklin which begins on page 234.

Step 1. Use your first color to highlight the first source listed on the list of Works Cited: the website article titled "Benjamin Franklin."

Step 2. Use that same color to highlight every citation that has the name "Benjamin" and every signal phrase that says *Bio.*

Step 3. Read carefully and color in the text of the essay so that everything from this source is colored with your first color.

Step 4. Use your second color to highlight the second source listed on the list of Works Cited: the article by James Dillon.

Step 5. Use that same color to highlight every citation and every signal phrases that has the name Dillon.

Step 6. Read carefully and color in the text of the essay so that everything from this source is colored with your second color.

Step 7. Use your third color to highlight the third source listed on the list of Works Cited: the encyclopedia article titled "Franklin, Benjamin."

Step 8. Use that same color to highlight every citation that has the name "Franklin" and every signal phrase that says *Brittanica.*

Step 9. Read carefully and color in the text of the essay so that everything from this source is colored with your third color.

Step 10. Use your fourth color to highlight the fourth source listed on the list of Works Cited: the book edited by Walter Isaacson.

Step 11. Use that same color to highlight every citation and every signal phrase that includes the name Isaacson.

Step 12. Read carefully and color in the text of the essay so that everything from this source is colored with your fourth color.

Look at the highlighted essay and notice that nearly everything is highlighted one of your four colors. The sentences that are not highlighted are the student's own thoughts and opinions. The in-text citations and signal phrases show the reader which information came from each source on the list of Works Cited.

Sixth Skill: Documenting Sources with a List of Works Cited

By themselves, in-text citations and signal phrases don't give much information. They just direct the reader to the Works Cited page which contains ALL the information about each source. The list of Works Cited is a **separate page** at the end of your paper. The sources on the page are listed in **alphabetical order.**

The official handbook for MLA documentation style gives directions and examples of every imaginable type of source you might ever need to cite in a research paper. The chapter on creating your list of Works Cited is thirty-two pages long. If you have an unusual situation for one of your sources, you can look it up in the *MLA Handbook* or on the website owl.english.purdue.edu.

The examples below cover the most common types of sources and situations that you will encounter in your research.

Books

Books are easy to cite because all the information you need is on the title page. The title page is one of the first pages at the very beginning of the book.

Information you will find for all books:

> Title
>
> Publishing Company
>
> Year when the book was published (copyright year)

Extra information you will find for some books but not others:

Subtitle

Author's name

Editor's name

Edition

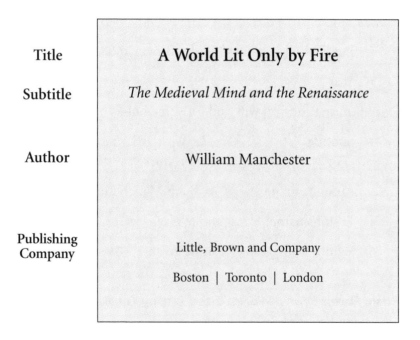

Title	**A World Lit Only by Fire**
Subtitle	*The Medieval Mind and the Renaissance*
Author	William Manchester
Publishing Company	Little, Brown and Company
	Boston | Toronto | London

This book does not have an editor or an edition. If it did, that information would be on the title page. Where's the **year of publication**? Sometimes the year is on the title page, but oftentimes you will have to turn the page and look at the back side of the title page to find the date. The date can be hard to find, but it's there. If you find more than one year, use the most recent year. That's the year when this particular copy of the book was printed.

Here's the information for this book:

Information you will need for all books:

Title	*A World Lit Only By Fire*
Publishing Company	Little, Brown and Company
Year	1992

Extra information you will find for some books but not others:

Subtitle	*The Medieval Mind and the Renaissance*
Author's name	William Manchester
Editor's name	none given
Edition	none given

Basic Format for a Works Cited Listing for Books

Author's last name, Author's first name. *Title: Subtitle.* Publishing Company, Year.

Works Cited Listing for the Book Shown Above

Manchester, William. *A World Lit Only By Fire: The Medieval Mind and the Renaissance.* Little, Brown, 1992.

Things to Notice

- The author's last name comes first, and then a comma, and then the first name.

- The title and subtitle are in italics with a colon (:) between them.

- The name of the publishing company has been shortened; we left off *and Company.*

- The first line of the listing is at the left margin. The second line is indented five spaces. (Just hit the TAB key one time to indent.) This format is called "hanging indent."

Basic Format for In-Text Citations for Books

(Author's last name page)

In-Text Citation for the Book Shown Above

(Manchester 53)

Things to Notice

- Only one empty space separates the author's last name from the page number. Don't put a comma or *pg.* or *page.*

Examples of Different Kinds of Book Entries

A Book with One Author

Author's last name, Author's first name. *Title: Subtitle.* Publishing Company, Year.

Kauffman, Michael W. *American Brutus: John Wilkes Booth and the Lincoln Conspiracies.* Random House, 2004.

In-Text Citation: (Kauffman 68).

A Book with Two Authors

For a book with more than one author, when you list the first author, put the last name first. When you list the other author, put the names in normal order.

Gies, Frances and Joseph Gies. *Life in a Medieval Village.*
Harper and Row, 1990.

In-Text Citation: (Gies and Gies 139).

A Book with Three or More Authors

For a book with three or more authors, give the first author's name (Last name first) and then write *et al. Et al* is Latin for "and others."

Okuda, Michael, et al. *The Star Trek Encyclopedia: A Reference Guide to the Future.* Pocket, 1994.

In-Text Citation: (Okuda et al 383).

A Book with an Unknown Author

If you don't know the author, skip that information and start your listing with the title. In the in-text citation, use a shortened version of the title. Be sure to italicize the title in your in-text citation to show that it is part of the title, not a crazy last name.

Title: Subtitle. Publisher, Year.

American Advertising 1800–1900. Chandler, 1988.

In-Text Citation: (*American* 12–14).

A Book That Has an Author and an Editor

If the title page gives an editor's name, put the name (in normal order) right after the title.

Author's last name, Author's first name. *Title: Subtitle.* Edited by Editor's name. Publishing Company, Year.

Shakespeare, William. *MacBeth.* Edited by Barbara A. Mowat and Paul Werstine. Simon and Schuster, 2009.

In-Text Citation: (Shakespeare 98–100)

A Book That Has an Editor but Not an Author

If the book has an editor but not an author, put the editor's name first, where the author's name would usually go.

Editor's last name, Editor's first name, editor. *Title: Subtitle.* Publishing Company, Year.

Suriano, Gregory R., editor. *Great American Speeches.* Gramercy, 1993.

In-Text Citation: (Suriano 3)

A Book That Has an Edition

If a book has been published more than once, the title page will say *Second Edition, Third Edition,* etc.

Author's last name, Author's first name. *Title: Subtitle.* Edition. Publishing Company, Year.

Aronson, Elliot. *The Social Animal.* 7th ed., Freeman, 1995.

In-Text Citation: (Aronson 97)

A Book with Articles or Chapters Written by Different Authors

Sometimes a book will be a collection of stories, articles, or chapters, and each section was written by a different author. In this case, you would treat each article or chapter that you use as a separate source.

Start your listing with the information about the specific article or chapter that you used, and then give the information about the book in which you read that article or chapter. After the year, put the page numbers for the article or chapter.

Author's last name, Author's first name. "Title of the Article or Chapter." *Title of the Whole Book: Subtitle,* edited by Editor's name. Publishing Company, Year, Pages.

Sitler, Robert K. "2012 and the Maya World." *The Mystery of 2012: Predictions, Prophecies, and Possibilities,* edited by Tami Simon, Sounds True, 2007, pp. 89–107.

In-Text Citation: (Sitler 101–6)

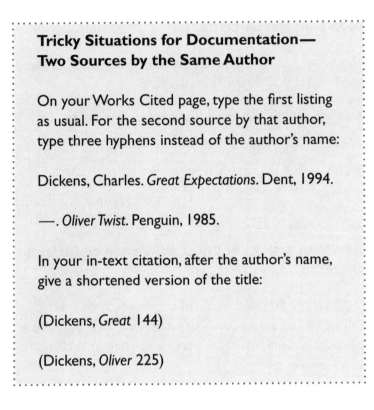

**Tricky Situations for Documentation—
Two Sources by the Same Author**

On your Works Cited page, type the first listing as usual. For the second source by that author, type three hyphens instead of the author's name:

Dickens, Charles. *Great Expectations*. Dent, 1994.

—. *Oliver Twist*. Penguin, 1985.

In your in-text citation, after the author's name, give a shortened version of the title:

(Dickens, *Great* 144)

(Dickens, *Oliver* 225)

Encyclopedias

Note: The information about encyclopedias given here is for big, general encyclopedias like *Encyclopedia Britannica, Colliers*, etc. For smaller or more specialized encyclopedias or reference books, follow the example given above for A Book with Articles or Chapters Written by Different Authors.

When you use an encyclopedia, you aren't using the whole book. You are using just one entry or article in the book. The title of the entry is the word you looked up to find that information.

No one person wrote the entire encyclopedia. Each entry was written by a different author. Sometimes you can tell who wrote that entry, but usually the author's name isn't given. If the author's name is given, it would be listed at the very end of the article or entry.

Encyclopedias are easy to cite because the information you need is in the entry you looked up or on the title page. The title page is one of the first pages at the very beginning of the book.

See page 243 for an example of a title page.

Information you can find for all encyclopedia entries:

Title of the entry or article

Title of the encyclopedia

Edition

Year when the book was published (copyright year)

Extra information you can find in some encyclopedias but not others:

Author's name

Title of Entry

> **Buckingham Palace**, residence of the British sovereigns from 1837, Westminster metropolitan borough, London, England, adjacent to St. James's Park. Built (1703) by the duke of Buckingham, it was purchased (1761) by George III and was remodeled (1825) by John Nash; the eastern façade was added in 1847. The great ballroom was added in 1856, and in 1913 Sir Anston Webb designed a new front. The palace has nearly 600 rooms and contains a collection of paintings, including many royal portraits, by noted artists.

Author (not given)

Here's the information for this entry:

Information you can find for all encyclopedia entries:

Title of the entry or article	"Buckingham Palace"
Title of the encyclopedia	*The Columbia Encyclopedia*
Edition	5th
Year	1993

Extra information you can find for some encyclopedias but not others:

Author's name	not given

Basic Format for a Works Cited Listing for an Encyclopedia Entry:

"Title of the Entry." *Title of the Encyclopedia.* Edition, Publishing Company, Year.

Works Cited Listing for the Book Shown Above:

"Buckingham Palace." *The Columbia Encyclopedia.* 5th ed., Columbia UP, 1993.

In-Text Citation for the Book Shown Above

("Buckingham")

Things to Notice

- Since we don't know who the author of this entry was, we skip that information and start with the title of the entry.

- The title of the entry is in quotation marks.

- The title of the encyclopedia is in italics.

- The edition comes after the title of the encyclopedia.

- The word in the in-text citation is a shortened version of the title of the entry. Be sure to put quotation marks around the word to show that it is part of the title, not an author's last name.

Since encyclopedias are arranged alphabetically, you don't need to put any page numbers in the Works Cited listing or in the in-text citation.

Magazine, Journal, and Newspaper Articles

When you cite an article from a magazine, newspaper, or other periodical, you first give the information about the article you used. Then you give information about the magazine or newspaper in which you read that article. You can find all this information either in the article or on the cover of the magazine or the front page of the newspaper.

Information you will find for all articles:

Title of the article

Title of the magazine or newspaper

Date when the magazine or newspaper was published

Extra information you will find for some articles but not others:

Author's name

Page numbers

Volume and issue numbers

Basic Format for a Works Cited Listing for Articles

Author's last name, Author's first name. "Title of the Article." *Title of the Magazine or Newspaper,* Date, Page numbers.

Sample Works Cited Listing for an Article

Keillor, Garrison. "There's No Place Like Home." *National Geographic,* Feb. 2014, pp. 58–83.

Things to Notice

- The author's last name comes first, and then a comma, and then the first name.

- The title of the article is in quotation marks.

- The title of the magazine is in italics.

- The month has been abbreviated. (*An abbreviation guide is on page 259.*)

- The letters *pp.* mean multiple pages. If the article is only one page long, just type p. which means page. Be careful to type only pp. or p., not pg. or pgs.

- The first line of the listing is at the left margin. The second line is indented five spaces. (Just hit the TAB key one time to indent.)

Basic Format for In-Text Citations for Articles

(Author's last name page)

In-Text Citation for the Article Shown Above

(Keillor 79–80)

Things to Notice

- Only one empty space separates the author's last name from the page number. Don't put a comma or *pg.* or *page.*

Examples of Different Kinds of Print Article Entries

Article in a Monthly Magazine

Shute, Nancy. "If We Only Had Wings." *National Geographic,* Sept. 2011, pp. 67–79.

In-Text Citation: (Shute 69)

Article in a Weekly Magazine

Alter, Jonathan. "With a Little Help From Our Kids."
Newsweek, 17 Nov. 2008, pp. 28–29.

In-Text Citation: (Alter 29)

Article in a Journal

A journal is a magazine that has a volume number and an issue number in addition to the date.

Author's last name, Author's first name. "Title of the Article."
Title of the Journal, Volume, Issue, Date, Pages.

Kaliss, Jeff. "Talkin' Shop." *Jazz Times,* vol. 22, no. 2, 1992,
pp. 24–27.

In-Text Citation: (Kaliss 25)

Article with an Unknown Author

If you don't know the author of the article, skip that information and begin with the title of the article. Use a shortened version of the title in your in-text citation. Be sure to put quotation marks around the word(s) in your in-text citation so that the reader knows that it is a title, not a crazy last name.

"Title of the Article." *Title of the Magazine,* Date, Pages.

"Beautiful Ruins." *Elle Décor,* Mar. 2014, p. 53.

In-Text Citation: ("Beautiful" 53)

Typing Page Numbers on Your Works Cited Page

Many newspapers have several sections with separate page numbers in each section. Section A may have page numbers 1-12; section B may have page numbers 1-8, etc. When you type the page number for a newspaper article, type the letter and then the page number with no punctuation or space in between:

Newspaper: A5

If the article is on several pages in a row, type the page number on which the article begins, then a hyphen, and then the page number on which the article ends.

Magazine: 15-18

Newspaper: C2-3

If the article begins on one page and then skips some pages and ends on another page, type the page number on which the article begins and then a plus sign to indicate that it has more pages later on in the magazine or newspaper:

Magazine: 27 +

Newspaper: A1 +

Article in a Newspaper

Author's last name, Author's first name. "Title of the Article." *Title of the Newspaper,* Date, Page.

Cave, Damien. "Migrants' New Paths Reshaping Latin America." *New York Times,* 6 Jan. 2012, p. A1.

In-Text Citation: (Cave A1)

A Newspaper Article with an Unknown Author

If you don't know the author of the article, skip that information and begin with the title of the article. Use a shortened version of the title in your in-text citation. Be sure to put quotation marks around the word(s) in your in-text citation so that the reader knows it is a title, not a crazy last name.

"Title of the Article." *Title of the Newspaper,* Date, Page.

"African Union Extends Somalia Force." *New York Times,* 6 Jan. 2012, p. A8.

In-Text Citation: ("African Union" A8).

Typing Months on Your Works Cited Page

Jan.	Apr.	July	Oct.
Feb.	May	Aug.	Nov.
Mar.	June	Sep.	Dec.

Editorial in a Magazine or Newspaper

"Donors, Secrecy and That Loophole." *New York Times,* 6 Jan.
2012, p. A22. Editorial.

> In-Text Citation: ("Donors" A22)

Letter to the Editor in a Magazine or Newspaper

Miller, Sheri. "Seeds for Change." *Mother Earth News,* Jan./
Feb. 2014, p. 10. Letter.

> In-Text Citation: (Miller 10)

Article in a Newspaper When the City is Not in the Title of the Newspaper

Most newspapers include the city name in the title of the newspaper: *New York Times, Boston Globe,* etc.

If you have a newspaper that does not have the city name in its
title, include the city name in your listing.

Author's last name, Author's first name. "Title of the Article."
Title of the Newspaper [City], Date, Page.

Tucker, John H. "A Time Bomb." *Indy Week* [Durham], 12
Feb. 2014, pp. 21–23.

> In-Text Citation: (Tucker 23)

Examples of Different Kinds of Online Article Entries

By using the internet and databases, you can access lots of articles that would be difficult or impossible to find in print. For each listing, you need to give information about the article first and then give information about the website or database where you found the article.

An Article in an Online Newspaper

Author's last name, Author's first name. "Title of the Article." *Title of the Newspaper*, Date, URL.

Trimble, James. "Bedroom Tax Help Too Late for Some in Falkirk." *The Falkirk Herald*, 16 Feb. 2014, www.falkirkherald.com/2014/216/bedroom-tax-help-too-late-for-some-in-falkirk.

In-Text Citation: (Trimble)

An Article in an Online Magazine

Author's last name, Author's first name. "Title of the Article." *Title of the Magazine*, Date, URL.

Hackett, Kathleen. "Creating a Scene: Cameron Diaz's Manhattan Apartment." *Elledecor*, 4 Oct. 2014, www.elledecor.com/celebrity-style/celebrity-homes/news/g498/cameron-diaz-manhattan-apartment/.

In-Text Citation: (Hackett)

Article from a Database

Most college libraries subscribe to one or more databases. A database allows you to search for and read all kinds of articles online.

The format for citing an article in a database is almost identical to the format for citing an article you read in print. The only difference is that you need to insert the name of the database right before the URL. Some databases include page numbers, but others don't.

Here is an example for a **magazine or newspaper article found in a database:**

Author's last name, Author's first name. "Title of the Article." *Title of the Magazine or Newspaper,* Date, Page. *Name of the Database,* URL.

"Two E. coli outbreaks in the last quarter of 2015." *Food Engineering,* Jan. 2016, p. 13. *Science in Context,* link.galegroup.com/apps/doc/A449928844/SCIC?u=nclive&xid=c017dbbc.

In-Text Citation: ("Two" 13)

Here is an example for a **journal article found in a database:**

Author's last name, Author's first name. "Title of the Article." *Title of the Journal,* Volume, Number, Date, Pages. *Name of the Database,* URL.

Murtaza, Ghulam. "Sherman Alexie's Discursive Reconstruction of the Native American Subject." *NUML Journal of Critical Inquiry*, vol. 14, no. 1, 2016, pp. 31-35. *ProQuest Central*, http://nclive.org/cgi-bin/nclsm?url=http://search. proquest.com/docview/1806173479?accountid=8241.

In-Text Citation: (Murtaza 34)

Websites

Websites can be tricky to cite because you may have difficulty finding the information you need. Try looking at the very top of the page and also at the very bottom of the page. If a website doesn't give some of the information, you can leave that information out.

Information you will need for all websites:

    Title of the website

Information to include if you have it:

    Author

    Sponsor of the site

    Date when the site was last updated

Basic Format for a Works Cited Listing for Websites

Author's last name, Author's first name. *Title of the Website.* Sponsor, date when the site was last updated, URL.

Silagy, Eric. *Energy Now.* Florida Power and Light, 31 May
    2015, www.nexteraenergy.com/energynow/
    2015/0515/0515_lp.shtml.

Things to Notice

- The author's last name comes first, and then a comma, and then the first name.

- The title of the website is in italics.

- The month has been abbreviated. *(An abbreviation guide is on page 259.)*

- The first line of the listing is at the left margin. The second line is indented five spaces. (Just hit the TAB key one time to indent.)

Basic Format for In-Text Citations for Websites

(Author's last name)

In-Text Citation for the Website Shown Above

(Silargy)

Things to Notice

- No page number is needed since websites don't have page numbers.

Examples of Different Kinds of Website Entries

An Entire Website

Follow this example when you used the whole website.

Author's last name, Author's first name. *Title of the Website.* Sponsor, date when the site was last updated, URL.

Jones, Allan Riley. *Gilbert and Sullivan Study Materials.* Arjentium, 2016, http://www.arjentium.com/index.php?pg= gs_study.

In-Text Citation: (Jones)

A Website with the Same Name as its Sponsor

When an organization makes a website, they often use the name of their organization for the name of their website. In this case, you should skip naming the sponsor so that you're not putting the same information twice:

"Why Animal Rights?" *PETA*, 2016, http://www.peta.org/about-peta/why-peta/why-animal-rights/.

In-Text Citation: ("Why")

Short Work from a Website

Follow this example when you are using one part of the website, not the entire website.

Author's last name, Author's first name. "Title of the Article or Part." *Title of the Website,* Sponsor, date when the site was last updated, URL.

Blaivas, Allan J. "Obstructive Sleep Apnea." *Medline Plus,* National Institutes of Health, 2 Dec. 2016, www.medline plus.gov/ency/article/000811.htm.

Just Skip It

If the website doesn't give the sponsor, just skip that information. If the website doesn't give the date when it was last updated, skip that information BUT instead give the date when you looked at the website after the URL.

Here's an example of a listing for a website that didn't give the sponsor or the date:

Wagner, Shirley. "The Moves Make the Man." *The Book Reviews Website,* www.thebook reviews.the-moves-makes-the-man. Accessed 16 Feb. 2014.

In-Text Citation: (Wagner)

Short Work from a Website with an Unknown Author

"John Lee Hooker." *Bio.*, A & E Television Networks, 2012,
   http://www.biography.com/people/john-lee-hooker-
   9343203.

In-Text Citation: ("John Lee Hooker")

Short Work from a Website When the Author is an Organization

American Wildlife Foundation. "The Great Fish River Rhino
   Conservation." *American Wildlife Foundation*, 13 Feb. 2014,
   www.awf.org/projects/great-fish-river-rhino-conservation.

Note: The sponsor for this website is left off because the sponsor's name is the same as the name of the website.

In-Text Citation for this Source: (American Wildlife)

Other Sources

Film, Video, or DVD

Title of the Movie. Directed by Director's Name, Performances
   by Names of the Major Performers, Distributor, Year.

The Apartment. Directed by Billy Wilder, Performances by
   Jack Lemmon, Shirley MacLaine, and Fred MacMurray,
   United Artists, 1960.

In-Text Citation: (*Apartment*).

Radio or Television Program

"Title of the Show or Episode." *Title of the Program,* Network, Date of Broadcast.

"Legal Scholar: Jim Crow Still Exists in America." *Fresh Air,* National Public Radio, 16 Jan. 2012.

In-Text Citation: ("Legal Scholar")

"The Cost." *The Wire,* HBO, 11 Aug. 2002.

In-Text Citation: ("Cost")

Personal Interview

If you can find a person who is knowledgeable about your topic, you could interview him or her and use the interview as one of your sources.

Last Name of the Person You Interviewed, First Name of the Person You Interviewed. Personal interview, Date of the Interview.

Johnson, Kenneth. Personal interview, 5 Sept. 2011.

In-Text Citation: (Johnson)

Exercise 10.8—Works Cited Listings and In-Text Citations

Write a Works Cited listing and an In-Text Citation for each of these sources. Check your answers on page 344.

1. The title of the book is *The Professor and the Madman*. It was published by Harper Collins in 1998. The author's name is Simon Winchester. You used a quote on page 88.

2. The title of the book is *Cutting Gardens*. It was published in 1993 by Simon and Shuster. The book was written by Anne Halpin and Betty Mackey. You used information from pages 58–60.

3. The article is from the January 2012 edition of the magazine *Smithsonian*. It was written by Eric Wagner. The title of the article is "Way of the Wolverine." The article is on pages 13–15. You used information from page 14.

4. This article was in the *New York Times* on Friday, January 6, 2012. The title of the article is "In East Africa, Towns Suffer in Crackdown on Diamonds." This article starts on page A4 and then skips ahead to page A8. You are using a quote taken from page A8. The article was written by John Eligon.

5. This article was in the *New York Times* on Friday, January 6, 2012. The title of the article is "Election Chief will not Resign." The author's name is not given. The entire article is on page A9.

6. This entry was in the print version of the fifth edition of *The Columbia Encyclopedia*. You were looking for information about the Isle of Man. The entry was listed as "Man, Isle of." The publisher is Columbia University Press, and it was published in 1993.

7. The name of the web site is *Audubon*. The name of the article you used is "Hummingbirds at Home: The Effect of Climate Change on Feeding Behavior." It doesn't say who wrote the article. The publisher of the web site is the National Audubon Society, and it was last updated in 2014. The URL is www.audubon.org/content/hummingbirds-home-effects-climate-change-feeding-behavior.

Exercise 10.9 Reviewing What You've Learned

Check your answers on page 345.

1. What are three things that you must think about when you evaluate sources for your research paper?

2. When you paraphrase, you must change the words that can be changed. Give an example of words that you would not be able to change.

3. Besides changing the words that can be changed, you must also change the _____ _____ when you paraphrase.

4. True or False? When you paraphrase, you can leave out any information that you don't think is important as long as you don't change the meaning of the original text.

5. True or False? It is best to do one sentence at a time when you are paraphrasing.

6. Approximately how many quotations should you have in a research paper?

7. Most of your quotations should be short, but what should you do if you need to include a quotation that is more than four lines long?

8. You need to include ellipses (...) to show that you left some words out of a quote only if

_____.

9. If you need to insert an explanation into a quote, what kind of punctuation should you put around the words you are inserting?

10. When you take notes, should each note be short or long?

11. What should you write at the top of each note?

12. What should you write at the end of each note?

13. True or False? It is fine to copy the exact words when you take notes as long as you put quotation marks around the words you copied.

14. You must put an in-text citation at the end of every sentence that includes a _____ and at the end of each section of _____.

15. You don't have to put a page number in the in-text citation if the source you are citing doesn't have

_____, such as a web site.

16. True or False? The number of in-text citations you have in your paper depends on how often you switched from one source to another and how many quotations you have.

17. How are in-text citations and signal phrases alike?

18. How are in-text citations and signal phrases different?

19. When would you need to use an in-text citation even though you already used a signal phrase?

Part Three: Using your Skills to Write a Research Paper Step-by-Step

Follow these steps to complete your research paper

Step 1: Do Preliminary Research

Step 2: Develop Your Research Question

Step 3: Find the Information You Need and Maintain a Working Bibliography

Step 4: Take Notes (Paraphrase, Summarize, and Quote)

Step 5: Sort Your Notes into Piles Based on the Key Words

Step 6: Rearrange Your Notes into a Skeleton Draft

Step 7: Smooth the Skeleton Draft into a Rough Draft

Step 8: Revise

Step 9: Remove Unnecessary In-Text Citations

Step 10: Edit

Step 11: Format

Step 12: Finish Your Paper and Celebrate!

Step 1: Do Preliminary Research

Doing research can seem like an overwhelming task. Where do you begin? If you type "Benjamin Franklin" into a search engine, you will have thirty-one million hits to sort through. By typing "Benjamin Franklin's Life" you will reduce the results to twenty-three million hits. Then there are the many books and articles about Franklin that can be found in public and college libraries. Obviously, sifting through all that information would take too long. You will need to **narrow your topic.**

To narrow your topic, start by doing **preliminary research:** look through encyclopedias, web sites, and other reference sources to get a general overview of your topic. Which aspects of the topic are most interesting to you? As Tiffany did her preliminary research for her paper on Benjamin Franklin, she noticed the many different types of work that Franklin did throughout his life. She decided to write about Franklin's many interests and present him as a multi-talented person.

Step 2: Develop Your Research Question

After you have narrowed your topic, the next step is to **develop a research question.** What question do you want to answer in your paper? Tiffany's research question was, "What different activities did Franklin work on at different times in his life?" At this point, it is a good idea to talk to your professor and get his or her approval for your topic and research question. Your professor can guide you in developing a question that will lead to a paper of the correct length.

Now you are ready to look for the information you will need to answer your research question.

Step 3: Find the Information You Need and Maintain a Working Bibliography

See pages 184–189 for directions on finding information to answer your research question.

As you do research, also create a **working bibliography.** A working bibliography is just a rough draft of your Works Cited page. Whenever you find a source that looks useful, list that source on your working bibliography. This will ensure that you have all the information that you will need later when you do the final draft of your Works Cited page. Nothing is more frustrating that having to go back to the library the day before your paper is due to try to find a source again because you forgot to write down the date when a book was published, etc. If you record detailed information on your working bibliography while you do your research, writing your list of Works Cited will be a breeze.

Pages 241–268 give information about what information you will need for every kind of source you may find.

Step 4: Take Notes

See pages 213–216 for instructions on taking notes.

Color-Coding Your Notes

Some students like to use colors to help them keep their notes organized. This can be done by using different colored index cards or different colored pens when you're taking notes.

Method #1: Use a different color for each of your sources. If you use yellow index cards for one source and blue for the next source and green for the third source, etc., you won't have to write the author's name in an in-text citation at the end of every note. For sources that don't have page numbers (such as internet sources), you wouldn't have to write an in-text citation at all. If you want to try this, be sure to keep track of which color goes with which source. You could simply write the colors by each source as you list it on your Working Bibliography.

Method #2: Use a different color for each key word. If you use a blue pen for the first key word, and a green pen for the second key word, and a red pen for the third key word, etc., you won't have to write the key words at the top of each note. Just keep a list of which color is for each key word.

Either of these methods will save you a little bit of time with note taking, and using colors can make note taking a little more fun.

Step 5: Sort Your Notes into Piles Based on the Key Words

After you finish taking your notes, you will need to sort them into piles based on the key word. Look at the key words at the top of each note and rearrange the notes to create a separate pile for each key word. (Everything about *childhood* goes in one pile; everything about *writing* goes in another pile, etc.)

- If you took notes on index cards, just sort the cards into separate piles for each key word.

- If you took notes on notebook paper, use scissors to cut the notes apart, and sort your slips of paper into piles.

- If you took notes directly onto the computer, high-light, cut, and paste to put the notes for each key word on a separate page of your document.

Time-Saving Tip:

Stop taking notes when you think you have about 75% of the information you need. If you continue taking notes until you feel like you're finished, you may have far more information than you can use in your paper. When you create your skeleton draft in Step 6, you may find that you don't need to take any more notes. If you do need to take more notes, you will see exactly what kind of information you still need to complete your paper.

Step 6: Rearrange Your Notes into a Skeleton Draft

Once you have a separate pile of cards or a separate page on the computer for each key word, you can work with one pile or one page at a time to create each paragraph. Rearrange the notes to put them into the right order to make a smooth paragraph.

You may find that you have similar information from several different sources. When Tiffany did her paper on Benjamin

Franklin, three of her sources said that Franklin died in 1790. When this happens, you can decide which source you want to use for that information. Eliminate any notes that you decide you don't need.

When you are finished rearranging the notes, you have the **skeleton** for your paper. All the information is in the right order (more or less) and all the in-text citations are in place.

Ah Ha!!

Now you can see why it was so important for you to write an in-text citation at the end of EVERY note. You can rearrange your notes again and again until you like the order, and the in-text citation travels with the notes, so you always know which source each note came from.

Step 7: Smooth the Skeleton Draft into a Rough Draft

If you wrote your notes on index cards or notebook paper, now is the time to type everything onto the computer. As you type, you can revise your wording to make the different bits of information into smooth sentences. Be sure to type in all the in-text citations as you go!

If you took notes on the computer, you can just reword for smoothness.

Step 8: Do Revision

Think about the following issues as you revise your rough draft:

- Content—is there anything that you should add or take out?

- Structure—does each body paragraph have a distinct main idea?

- Clarity—does anything need to be reworded so that the reader understands easily?

- Sentence Variety—do you have a nice blend of different kinds of sentences?

- Transitions—have you used transitions to guide the reader?

- Word Choice—have you used vivid words and active verbs as much as possible?

Step 9: Remove Unnecessary In-Text Citations

First Example: Essay with In-Text Citations Only

In-text citations show your reader which source every bit of information came from. You need an in-text citation at the end of every sentence that includes a **quotation** and at the end of every section of **paraphrased or summarized information.**

You might want to look back at the sample essay on pages 217–222 to remind yourself about the correct placement of in-text citations.

Look at the paragraph below and try to determine which in-text citations should be taken out:

Franklin worked at several different jobs in Philadelphia including bookkeeping, shop keeping, and printing ("Benjamin"). Finally, in 1728, he and a partner started their own print shop. ("Benjamin"). Around 1729 he began publishing a newspaper called the *Pennsylvania Gazette,* and in 1732 he started a series of magazines called *Poor Richard's Almanac* ("Franklin"). He used the pen name Richard Saunders and wrote articles "praising prudence [wisdom], industry [hard work], and honesty" ("Franklin"). These articles use a humorous tone to offer common sense advice to readers (Isaacson, 124). In one article titled "Reasons to Choose an Older Mistress," Franklin describes eight reasons why it is better to date an older woman than a young woman (Isaacson, 125). His final argument is " … they are so grateful!!" (qtd. in Isaacson 125). Not quite following his own advice, Franklin married a young woman named Deborah Read ("Benjamin"). They were married for forty-four years and had three children ("Benjamin").

Here is the same paragraph with the extra in-text citations removed:

> Franklin worked at several different jobs in Philadelphia including bookkeeping, shop keeping, and printing. Finally, in 1728, he and a partner started their own print shop ("Benjamin"). Around 1729 he began publishing a newspaper called the *Pennsylvania Gazette,* and in 1732 he started a series of magazines called *Poor Richard's Almanac.* He used the pen name Richard Saunders and wrote articles "praising prudence [wisdom], industry [hard work], and honesty" ("Franklin"). These articles use a humorous tone to offer common sense advice to readers. In one article titled "Reasons to Choose an Older Mistress," Franklin describes eight reasons why it is better to date an older woman than a young woman. His final argument is " … they are so grateful!!" (qtd. in Isaacson 125). Not quite following his own advice, Franklin married a young woman named Deborah Read. They were married for forty-four years and had three children ("Benjamin").

Second Example: Essay with In-Text Citations and Signal Phrases

In-text citations and signal phrases show your reader which source every bit of information came from. You need an in-text citation or signal phrase for each **quotation** and for each section of **paraphrased or summarized information**.

You might want to look back at the sample essay on pages 234–239 to remind yourself about the correct placement of in-text citations and signal phrases.

Look at the paragraph below and try to determine which in-text citations and signal phrases should be taken out:

(Remember that "Franklin" is the title of the article in Encyclopedia Britannica and "Benjamin" is the title of the article on the Bio website.)

Britanica details Franklin's work as a diplomat between 1757 and 1775 ("Franklin"). Franklin was selected to represent the interests of Pennsylvania and several other colonies in England, so he spent several years living in London working to promote the colonies' interests with the English government ("Franklin"). In 1775, seeing that there could soon be a war between England and the colonies, Franklin returned home ("Franklin"). *Bio* describes how Franklin played an important role in the fight for independence and the development of a new government for the young United States of America ("Benjamin"). He served as a delegate to the Second Continental Congress, was one of the five men who wrote the Declaration of Independence, and was one of the thirteen who wrote the Articles of Confederation ("Benjamin"). At the beginning of the Revolutionary War, Franklin travelled to France to ask the French government to help the colonies by providing money and military assistance ("Franklin"). In 1783, after the Revolutionary War ended, Franklin and several other diplomats negotiated the peace treaty with England ("Benjamin").

Here is the same paragraph with the unnecessary in-text citations and signal phrases removed:

Britanica details Franklin's work as a diplomat between 1757 and 1775. Franklin was selected to represent the interests of Pennsylvania and several other colonies in England, so he spent several years living in London working to promote the colonies' interests with the English government. In 1775, seeing that there could soon be a war between England and the colonies, Franklin returned home. *Bio* describes how Franklin played an important role in the fight for independence and the development of a new government for the young United States of America. He served as a delegate to the Second Continental Congress, was one of the five men who wrote the Declaration of Independence, and was one of the thirteen who wrote the Articles of Confederation ("Benjamin"). At the beginning of the Revolutionary War, Franklin travelled to France to ask the French government to help the colonies by providing money and military assistance ("Franklin"). In 1783, after the Revolutionary War ended, Franklin and several other diplomats negotiated the peace treaty with England ("Benjamin").

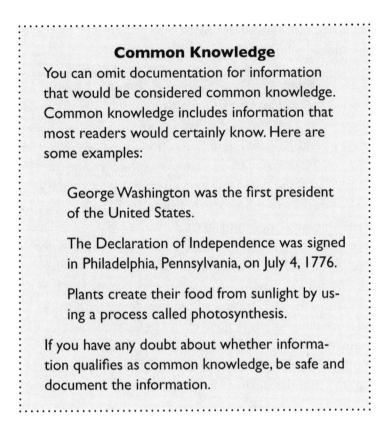

Common Knowledge

You can omit documentation for information that would be considered common knowledge. Common knowledge includes information that most readers would certainly know. Here are some examples:

George Washington was the first president of the United States.

The Declaration of Independence was signed in Philadelphia, Pennsylvania, on July 4, 1776.

Plants create their food from sunlight by using a process called photosynthesis.

If you have any doubt about whether information qualifies as common knowledge, be safe and document the information.

Step 10: Edit

Think about the following issues as you edit your revised draft:

- Have you fixed any fragments, comma splices, or run-ons?

- Have you used commas, semi-colons, colons, dashes, and apostrophes correctly?

- Are all the quotation marks in the right places?

- Do all your verbs agree with their subjects?

- Are all your pronouns clear and do they agree with their antecedents?

- Do you have any misplaced or dangling modifiers?

- Are there any problems with parallel structure?

- Have you used the correct words and spelled them all correctly?

Step 11: Formatting

Formatting is more complicated with a research essay. First consider the issues you have with formatting any essay:

- Margins should be one inch all the way around

- **Everything** should be double spaced

- Paragraphs should be indented five spaces

- Type your last name and the page number at the top of each page at the right margin

- Type your heading on the first page only, at the left margin

Your name	Tiffany Bradshaw
Professor's name	Professor Anders
Class	English 111
Date the paper is due	16 April 2017

Here are extra formatting considerations for a research paper:

- Long quotes (more than four lines of typing) should be indented ten spaces from the left margin to make a blocked quote.

- Don't put quotation marks around blocked quotes.

- At the end of a blocked quote, put the period that ends the sentence **before** the in-text citation.

- In every other case, put the period that ends the sentence **after** the in-text citation.

- The list of Works Cited should be a separate page at the end of your essay.

- The sources on your list of Works Cited should be in alphabetical order.

- For each source listed, the first line should be at the left margin, and the subsequent lines should be indented five spaces. This is called hanging indentation.

You can look at the sample essay on pages 234–239 to see how a correctly formatted research paper should look.

Step 12: Finish Your Paper and Celebrate!

Writing a research paper is a lot of work. After you turn your paper in, reward yourself. You have earned it!

Appendix

✧

Types of Verbs

Verbs can be divided into three groups: **action verbs, linking verbs,** and **helping verbs.**

An **ACTION VERB** is a word that tells what somebody does:

Josh <u>ate</u> corn flakes for breakfast.

Eating is an action, so *ate* is an action verb.

A **LINKING VERB** tells what somebody or something is:

The roses <u>are</u> pink.

Do the roses have to do anything to be pink? No. They just are pink. So *are* is a linking verb.

All the forms of the verb *to be* are always linking verbs: am, is, are, was, were, will be. A few other words can be action verbs or linking verbs depending on the sentence:

> The rose <u>smelled</u> good.   Linking verb
> Tenisha <u>smelled</u> the rose.   Action verb

In the first sentence, the rose didn't do anything. It just has a fragrance that smells good, so *smelled* is a linking verb. In the second sentence, Tenisha bent down over the rose and sniffed to smell the rose. Tenisha performed an action, so in this sentence *smelled* is an action verb.

A **HELPING VERB** works with a main verb to show complicated tenses or times. **Verb phrases** (two or more words working together as the verb) tell when one thing happened in relationship to something else:

> Before the party began, he <u>had drunk</u> the lemonade. (past perfect)

> He <u>has drunk</u> three glasses of lemonade already. (present perfect)

> He <u>will have drunk</u> all the lemonade before the cookies are served. (future perfect)

> When I arrived, he <u>was drinking</u> lemonade. (past progressive)

> He <u>is drinking</u> lemonade right now. (present progressive)

He <u>will be drinking</u> lemonade all afternoon. (future progressive)

He <u>had been drinking</u> lemonade all afternoon. (past perfect progressive)

He <u>has been drinking</u> lemonade all afternoon. (present perfect progressive)

He <u>will have been drinking</u> lemonade all afternoon. (future perfect progressive)

In these sentences, we see several different helping verbs being used with the main verbs **drunk** and **drinking**.

Note: An ING word will never be a verb by itself. But it can be part of a verb phrase as long as one or more helping verbs come before it.

Common Helping Verbs

am	**is**	**are**	**was**	**were**	**will**	**could**
be	**been**	**had**	**has**	**have**	**shall**	**would**

Notice that not all of the words in the verb phrase will change when we change the tense.

Yesterday He **had** drunk the lemonade.
Every day He **has** drunk the lemonade.
Tomorrow He **will have** drunk the lemonade.

The helping verb *had* changes when we change the time, but the main verb *drunk* does not change. This can make it tricky to know exactly which words to mark as the entire verb.

So do this: if you are marking verbs and you notice that the word that changes is on the list of helping verbs, look to see if the next word in the sentence is working with the helping verb to make a verb phrase.

Why does this matter? For practical grammar—what you need to know to write correctly—it doesn't matter. Each sentence you write needs a verb, and you can make sure you have a verb by changing the time. Even though not all the words in a complicated verb phrase will change, at least one of them will change, and that will indicate the verb.

Transitive and Intransitive Verbs

Verbs can also be classified as **transitive** or **intransitive**. A transitive verb takes a **direct object**, and an intransitive verb does not. Most verbs can be either transitive or intransitive depending on the sentence:

The <u>wind</u> <u>blew</u>.	Intransitive
The <u>wind</u> <u>blew</u> my **hat** off.	Transitive

In the second sentence, we have a direct object *hat*, so the verb *blew* is transitive in that sentence. For an explanation of direct objects, see page 297.

Verbals—Gerunds and Infinitives

A **GERUND** is a word that looks like a verb, but it has ING on the end, and it is not functioning as the verb in the sentence:

> Jill loves dancing.
> *Yesterday* Jill **loved** dancing.
> *Tomorrow* Jill **will love** dancing.

The word that changed is *loves,* so *loves* is the verb. *Dancing* tells what she loves. *Dancing* is a **direct object**. For an explanation of direct objects, see page 297.

Why isn't *loves dancing* a verb phrase? *Loves* is not one of the helping verbs. *Dancing* could be part of a verb phrase if it had a helping verb:

> Jill was dancing.

A gerund can also be the subject of a sentence:

> Dancing is good exercise.

An **INFINITIVE** is the word *to* followed by a verb. An infinitive does not function as the verb in a sentence:

> Jill loves to dance.
> *Yesterday* Jill **loved** to dance.
> *Tomorrow* Jill **will love** to dance.

The word that changed is *loves,* so *loves* is the verb. *To dance* tells what she loves. *To dance* is a **direct object**.

An infinitive can sometimes be the subject of a sentence:

To dance on Broadway is Jill's dream.

Tricky Sentence Structures

In most sentences, the subject will come before the verb. Here are some unusual sentences in which the subject comes after the verb.

An **EXPLETIVE** is a sentence that starts with *there:*

There is a fly in my soup!

Finding the verb is easy: *is.* But if I ask the subject question—"Who or what is a fly in my soup?"—I am liable to answer *there,* and *there* will never be the subject.

In an expletive, the subject will come after the verb. Follow these steps to find the subject:

There is a fly in my soup!

Step 1)   Eliminate the word *there:* Is a fly in my soup!

Step 2)   Rearrange the remaining words: A fly is in my soup!

Step 3)   Ask the subject question, "Who or what is in my soup?" *Fly.*

Step 4)   Mark the verb and subject in the original sentence: There is a fly in my soup!

Here's another example. The verb is *are*. Follow the steps to find the subject.

There <u>are</u> two cupcakes left.

Step 1) Eliminate the word *there*: <u>Are</u> two cupcakes left.

Step 2) Rearrange the remaining words: Two cupcakes <u>are</u> left.

Step 3) Ask the subject question, "Who or what are left?" *Cupcakes.*

Step 4) Mark the verb and subject in the original sentence: There <u>are</u> two <u>cupcakes</u> left.

In an **INTERROGATIVE** sentence (a question) the subject will often come in the middle of a verb phrase. Read about verb phrases on page 288 before you try to find the verbs in questions.

Did Sally eat the last piece of cake?
How much cake did Sally eat?

To find the verb and subject in a question, you first have to rewrite the question as a regular sentence by rearranging the words. Be sure to use exactly the same words:

Sally did eat the last piece of cake.
Sally did eat how much cake.

Now you can use the regular process to find the verb and the subject.

Every day Sally **does eat** the last piece of cake.
Tomorrow Sally **will eat** the last piece of cake.
"Who or what eats the last piece of cake?" *Sally.*

Every day Sally **does eat** how much cake.
Tomorrow Sally **will eat** how much cake.
"Who or what eats how much cake?" *Sally*

Mark the subject and verb in the original sentence:

<u>Did</u> <u>Sally</u> <u>eat</u> the last piece of cake?
How much cake <u>did</u> <u>Sally</u> <u>eat</u>?

An **IMPERATIVE** sentence is a command:

Scott's mom: "Pick up your dirty clothes."

This sentence does not name the person who needs to pick up the clothes because the name is not necessary. When Scott finishes taking a shower and leaves his dirty clothes all over the bathroom floor, he knows who his mom means when she says, "Pick up your dirty clothes." Scott understands that his mom means YOU (him), so we would say that the subject of this sentence is the **understood you.**

Shannon's roommate: "Please turn the music down."

The verb is *turn.* "Who or what should turn the music down?" The name is not given, but Shannon knows who her roommate means because Shannon is the one playing loud music while her roommate is trying to study. Shannon understands that her roommate means YOU (her).

To mark this type of sentence, write the word *you* in parentheses so that you can underline it as the subject:

> (<u>You</u>) <u>Turn</u> the music down.
> (<u>You</u>) <u>Pick up</u> your dirty clothes.

Sometimes a writer will place the subject after the verb in order to create a **DRAMATIC STYLE**. Finding the verb in this type of sentence can be challenging:

> Out of the hole ran the mouse.

You might want to begin by putting parentheses around the prepositional phrase in this sentence. Since the subject and verb will never be part of a prepositional phrase, eliminating those phrases will make the sentence shorter and easier to work with.

> (Out of the hole) ran the mouse.
> *Every day* **runs** the mouse.
> *Tomorrow* **will run** the mouse.

To find the subject, ask the usual question but stop right after you say the verb. Don't read all the way to the end of the sentence.

> "Who or what ran?" *Mouse*
> Out of the hole <u>ran</u> the <u>mouse</u>.

Analyzing sentences like this is mostly a matter of logic. There's really only one word in this sentence that could be a verb: *ran*. There are really only two words that could be the subject: *hole* or *mouse*. The hole can't run, so the subject must be *mouse*.

> ### Why does this matter?
>
> For practical grammar, it doesn't matter. You can write dramatic sentences in your papers without having to underline the subject and verb. Just be sure that your sentence isn't a fragment, comma splice, or run-on.

Clause Patterns

Direct Objects, Indirect Objects, Object Complements, and Subject Complements

When you're looking at clause patterns, take each clause of the sentence separately and disregard any phrases.

First Clause Pattern: S–V

<u>Subject</u> – <u>Verb</u>

> <u>Snakes</u> <u>bite</u>.
> <u>Maria</u> <u>drove</u> to the store.
> <u>Tom</u> and <u>Sue</u> <u>dined</u> and <u>danced</u> at the Ritz.

Second Clause Pattern: S–V–DO

<u>Subject</u> – <u>Verb</u> – **Direct Object**

To identify a **direct object**, say the subject and the verb, then ask, "what?" Direct objects only answer the question "what?" If a word is answering a different question, such as how or where, it is not a direct object.

<u>Snakes</u> <u>bite</u> **people.**
"Snakes bite what?" **People**

<u>Maria</u> <u>drove</u> her **car** to the store.
"Maria drove what?" **Car**

<u>Tom</u> and <u>Sue</u> <u>ate</u> **dinner** at the Ritz.
"Tom and Sue ate what?" **Dinner**

A **gerund** or an **infinitive** can also serve as a direct object:

<u>Jackie</u> <u>loves</u> **baking** brownies.
"Jackie loves what?" **Baking**

<u>Mark</u> <u>wants</u> **to win** the trophy.
"Mark wants what?" **To win**

Third Clause Pattern: S–V–IO–DO

<u>Subject</u> – <u>Verb</u> – Indirect Object – **Direct Object**

The indirect object receives the direct object.

<u>Steve</u> <u>gave</u> Jackie a new **car** for her birthday.
"Steve gave what?" **Car**
"Who received the car?" Jackie

<u>Jackie</u> <u>bought</u> Steve a **tie.**
"Jackie bought what?" **Tie**
"Who received the tie?" <u>Steve.</u>

<u>Chris</u> <u>offered</u> Stefan a **ride** in his plane.
"Chris offered what?" **Ride**
"Who received the ride?" <u>Stefan</u>

Fourth Clause Pattern: S–V–DO–OC

<u>Subject</u> – <u>Verb</u> – **Direct Object** – *Object Complement*

The object complement is a noun or adjective that modifies the direct object.

The <u>potion</u> <u>made</u> **Snow White** *sleepy.*
"The potion made what?" **Snow White**
"Word that describes Snow White?" *Sleepy*

<u>Love</u> <u>makes</u> a **house** a *home.*
"Love makes what?" **House**
"Word that describes house?" *Home*

Guinevere <u>found</u> **Hector** *annoying.*
"Guinevere found what?" **Hector**
"Word that describes Hector?" *Annoying*

Fifth Clause Pattern: S–LV–SC (PA/PN)

<u>Subject</u> -- <u>Linking Verb</u> – SUBJECT COMPLEMENT

The first four clause patterns are for clauses with action verbs. This is the pattern for a clause with a **linking verb.** See page 287 for information about linking verbs.

The subject complement is either a **predicate adjective (PA)** or a **predicate noun (PN).** It modifies the subject. See pages 305 and 309 for an explanation of nouns and adjectives.

<u>I</u> <u>am</u> HUNGRY.
"Word that describes the subject I?"   HUNGRY
"Is HUNGRY a noun or an adjective?"   Adjective.
So this clause is S–LV–SC (PA)

<u>I</u> <u>am</u> a POINT GUARD.
"Word that describes the subject I?" POINT GUARD
"Is POINT GUARD a noun or an adjective?" Noun.
So this clause is S–LV–SC (PN)

The <u>flowers</u> <u>were</u> BEAUTIFUL.
"Word that describes flowers?" BEAUTIFUL.
"Is BEAUTIFUL a noun or an adjective?" Adjective.
So this clause is S–LV–SC (PA)

Relative Clauses

The most common types of clauses are independent and dependent clauses. An **independent clause** has a subject and a verb, and it expresses a complete idea:

> Ty Jenkins averages fifty points a game.
>   IC

A **dependent clause** begins with a **subordinating conjunction** that changes the sound of the clause making it sound unfinished:

> Because Ty Jenkins averages fifty points a game . . .
>   DC

A **relative clause** begins with a relative word. The relative word takes the place of the subordinating conjunction and sometimes it also replaces the subject.

> Who averages fifty points a game
>   RC

In this clause, the verb is *averages*. *Who* is the relative word. In this sentence it is replacing both the subject and the subordinating conjunction. This clause would be complete if it were asking a question. But as a statement, it does not express a complete idea; consequently, a relative clause functions like a dependent clause. It depends on another clause.

Relative clauses often appear in the middle of another clause:

> Ty Jenkins, *who averages fifty points a game*, is a first round draft choice.

The relative clause gives useful information, but the independent clause could stand alone:

> Ty Jenkins is a first round draft choice.

Common Relative Words

who	**whose**	**which**
why	**where**	**that**

Here's another sentence with a relative clause in the middle of an independent clause:

> Sylvester the Cat, *whose determination exceeds his cleverness,* never catches Tweety Bird.

The independent clause is

> Sylvester the Cat never catches Tweety Bird.

In the relative clause, the relative word *whose* is replacing the subordinating conjunction

> whose determination exceeds his cleverness

Relative clauses can also come after an independent clause:

> I returned to the town *where I grew* up.
> Kari wondered *why her car's battery was* dead.
> Jacob had to decide *which computer was* best.
> He chose the computer *that had the most memory.*

For analyzing sentence types, count relative clauses as dependent clauses. If a sentence has an independent clause and a relative clause, it is complex.

For more on sentence types, see Chapter 9 beginning on page 161.

Kinds of Phrases

There are six kinds of phrases: **infinitive, appositive, prepositional, gerund, participial,** and **absolute.**

An **INFINITIVE PHRASE** begins with an **infinitive:** the word *to* followed by a verb. See page 291 for an explanation of infinitives.

> Steve wanted *to go skiing.*
> *To avoid the rain* Jill decided to stay home.

An **APPOSITIVE PHRASE** renames someone. See page 73 for more info on appositives. The following sentence names the woman once as *my sister* and then names her a second time as *the woman on crutches.*

> My sister, *the woman on crutches,* broke her leg skiing.

A **PREPOSITIONAL PHRASE** begins with a **preposition** and ends with a noun or pronoun. A preposition is something a cat can do with a chair. See page 308 for more information on prepositions.

> That painting *of the ocean* is beautiful.
> The gerbil ran *under the bed.*

A **GERUND PHRASE** begins with a **gerund**, a verb form ending with ING that functions as a noun. In the following sentence the gerund *opening* is a noun serving as the subject of the sentence. See page 291 for more information on gerunds.

See page 305 for an explanation of nouns.

Opening this door is so difficult.

A **PARTICIPIAL PHRASE** begins with a **participle**, a verb form ending with ING that functions as an adjective. In the following sentence the participle *wagging* is modifying the noun *dog.* See page 309 for an explanation of adjectives.

The dog *wagging its tail* is so friendly.

An **ABSOLUTE PHRASE** includes a noun followed by a participle. An absolute phrase is independent from the rest of the sentence.

The train having stopped, we gathered our luggage.

Do you need to know all these different types of phrases?

NO! For punctuation, all phrases are created equal.

Just follow the directions in Chapter 4 regarding introductory material, non-essential elements, etc. It doesn't matter what kind of phrase you're dealing with.

Parts of Speech

There are eight parts of speech: **verb, noun, pronoun, conjunction, preposition, adjective, interjection,** and **adverb.** Look for the parts of speech in this order, and you can use the process of elimination to identify the more difficult parts of speech. A dictionary will tell you what parts of speech a word can be. Many words can be different parts of speech depending on the job they are doing in a particular sentence.

Verbs

Verbs are very flexible and versatile. A verb may take many different forms to express action or state of being, number, and time.

Floyd **ate** the pizza.	Action
Pizza **is** delicious.	State of being
Jason **eats** pizza for breakfast.	Singular
All the guys **eat** pizza for breakfast.	Plural
Yesterday Sherry **ate** pizza.	Past
Every day Sherry **eats** pizza.	Present
Tomorrow Sherry **will eat** pizza.	Future

To find the verb of a sentence, use the time words—*yesterday, every day, tomorrow*—to change the time of the sentence. The word that changes when you change the time is the verb. Mark verbs with a <u>double underline</u>.

After he <u>jogged</u> briskly around the park, Mark <u>went</u> to the nearby Starbucks and <u>had</u> a Chai Tea.

For more on verbs, see Chapter 1.

Nouns

A **noun** is a person, place, thing, or idea. The subject of a sentence will often be a noun, but a sentence may have many other nouns too.

When you are analyzing a sentence for parts of speech, first find the verbs. Then look at the rest of the words and ask yourself if each word is the name of a person, place, thing, or idea. Mark the nouns with N:

> After he <u>jogged</u> briskly around the park, Mark <u>went</u>
>   N   N
>
> to the nearby Starbucks and <u>had</u> a chai tea.
>   N   N

Pronouns

A **pronoun** takes the place of a noun. A pronoun may be the subject of a sentence, or it may perform some other job. Mark pronouns as PN:

Pronouns

I	he	she	we	they	it
me	him	her	us	them	you

Note that possessive pronouns (my, mine, his, her, hers, your, our, their, etc.) function as adjectives. See page 310.

> After he <u>jogged</u> briskly around the park, Mark <u>went</u>
>   PN   N   N
>
> to the nearby Starbucks and <u>had</u> a chai tea.
>   N   N

Conjunctions

There are two kinds of conjunctions: **coordinating conjunctions** and **subordinating conjunctions.**

Coordinating Conjunctions

For   And   Nor   But   Or   Yet   So

There are only seven **coordinating conjunctions**, and they are all short words, only two or three letters long. You can use the acronym FANBOYS to remember them.

Mark coordinating conjunctions CC.

Common Subordinating Conjunctions

after	**although**	**as**	**because**
before	**if**	**since**	**so that**
that	**though**	**till**	**until**
unless	**when**	**where**	**while**

A **subordinating conjunction** is the first word of a clause, and it makes the clause dependent.

> Francesca <u>makes</u> her own jewelry.

This is a clause because it has a subject and a verb. It is an independent clause because it expresses a complete idea. If you put a subordinating conjunction at the beginning of the clause, the clause will become dependent:

> *Because* <u>Francesca</u> <u>makes</u> her own jewelry . . . WHAT?

Now this clause sounds unfinished. The subordinating conjunction *because* changed the sound of a clause and made the clause dependent.

Some of the words on the list of subordinating conjunctions can also do other jobs. If the word is truly a subordinating conjunction, it will come at the beginning of a clause and make the clause dependent.

See page 168 for false subordinating conjunctions.

Mark subordinating conjunctions with a wavy underline.

> <u>After</u> he <u>jogged</u> briskly around the park, Mark <u>went</u>
> SC   PN   N   N
>
> to the nearby Starbucks and <u>had</u> a chai tea.
>   N   CC   N

Interjections

Interjections are rare, but they are very easy to find. An interjection is a word such as *Oh, Wow, No, Yes,* or *Gosh.* An interjection would be the first word of a sentence. Mark interjections as I.

Gosh, I <u>love</u> grammar!
  I   PN   N

See page 65 for information on using commas with interjections.

Prepositions

A **preposition** tells what a cat can do with a chair.

A cat can be	**in** the chair
	under the chair
	beside the chair
	near the chair
	by the chair
	with the chair
A cat can jump	**over** the chair
	on the chair
	into the chair
	off the chair
	from the chair
A cat can run	**around** the chair
	to the chair
	through the legs of the chair
A cat can be so still that it looks like part	**of** the chair

Other prepositions include **about, along, at, beyond, beneath, between, for, like,** and more. You can look in a dictionary to see if a word can be a preposition.

A **prepositional phrase** begins with a preposition and then has another word or two or three to finish the idea. The last word of the prepositional phrase is always a noun or pronoun that is called the **object of the preposition.** Mark prepositions as PR and put parentheses around the entire prepositional phrase.

> After he jogged briskly (around the park), Mark
> SC   PN   PR   N   N

> went (to the nearby Starbucks) and had a chai tea.
> PR   N   CC   N

Adjectives

An **adjective** is a word that modifies or describes a noun. Adjectives answer the questions "How many? What kind? Which one?" In English, the adjective comes before the noun it describes. Mark adjectives ADJ.

Three special adjectives are the words *a, an,* and *the.* These are called **articles,** and they are always adjectives.

> After he jogged briskly (around the park,)Mark
> SC   PN   PR   ADJ   N   N

> went (to the nearby Starbucks) and had a chai
> PR ADJ   ADJ   N   CC   ADJ ADJ

> tea.
> N

The and *a* are articles, so those are automatically adjectives. *Nearby* answers "Which one?" about the Starbucks. *Chai* answers "What kind?" about the tea.

Another type of word that is always an adjective is a **possessive noun or pronoun**; it answers the adjective question "Which one?"

> That is *Susan's* purse.
> That is *her* purse.

Susan owns the purse. The word *Susan's* seems as if it would be a noun because it is her name. But her name is *Susan,* not *Susan's*. In the second sentence, *her* is a possessive pronoun also telling "Which one?" about the purse.

Possessive Pronouns

my	**your**	**their**	**her**	**his**
mine	**yours**	**theirs**	**hers**	**its**

Adverbs

Adverbs are the hardest part of speech to find. That is why we save them for last. When you have found the first seven parts of speech, any words left over are probably adverbs.

Mark adverbs as ADV.

Adverbs answer the questions "How? When? How much?" Adverbs can modify or describe verbs, adjectives, and other adverbs. First let's look at adverbs modifying verbs:

Bill <u>ate</u> quickly.
  N   ADV

Quickly answers "how?" about the verb *ate.*

Bill <u>ate</u> most (of his dinner).
  N   ADV PR ADJ   N

Most answers "how much?" about the verb *ate.*

Bill <u>jumped</u> high.
  N   ADV

High answers "how much?" about the verb *jumped.*

Yesterday, Bill <u>broke</u> his arm.
  ADV   N   ADJ N

Yesterday answers "when?" about the verb *broke.*

Bill <u>left</u> the party early.
  N   ADJ   N   ADV

Early answers "when?" about the verb *left.*

The word *not* is also an adverb that modifies a verb. *Not* will often come in the middle of a verb phrase, but it isn't a verb. It's an adverb. *Not* negates the verb.

Bill <u>did</u> not <u>brush</u> his teeth.
  N   ADV   ADJ N

Not negates the verb *did brush*

Adverbs can also modify or describe adjectives.

Bill <u>has</u> a light blue jacket.
  N   ADJ ADV ADJ   N

It is very tempting to mark *light* as an adjective that describes the jacket, but really *light* is answering "what kind?" about the adjective *blue*. Because *light* is modifying *blue*, and *blue* is an adjective, *light* must be an adverb. Don't let this mess you up with the article words, though *(a, an, the)*. Articles are always adjectives.

> Bill <u>has</u> a very old car.
> N　　ADJ ADV ADJ　N
>
> *Very* is answering "how much?" about the adjective
> *old. Old* describes the car, and *very* describes *old.*

Last but not least, an **adverb** can modify or describe another adverb.

> Bill <u>runs</u>　very quickly.
> N　　　　ADV　ADV
>
> *Quickly* answers "how?" about the verb *runs.*
> *Very* answers "how much?" about the adverb *quickly.*

In the next sentence, *briskly* answers "how?" about the verb *jogged:*

> <u>After</u> he <u>jogged</u> briskly (around the park),
> SC　PN　　　　　ADV　　　PR　ADJ　N
>
> Mark <u>went</u> (to the nearby Starbucks) and
> N　　　　PR ADJ　ADJ　　　　N　　　CC
>
> <u>had</u> a chai tea.
> ADJ ADJ　N

Answers

✧

Exercise 1.1 Finding Verbs

1. My neighbor George <u>loves</u> gardening.
    Tomorrow My neighbor George <u>will love</u> gardening.
2. Every weekend he <u>works</u> in his yard.
    Tomorrow Every weekend he <u>will work</u> in his yard.
3. George <u>went</u> on-line and <u>ordered</u> six apple trees.
    Every day George <u>goes</u> on-line and <u>orders</u> six apple trees.
4. The trees <u>came</u> in the mail in a large cardboard box; they <u>were</u> only three feet tall.
    Every day The trees <u>come</u> in the mail in a large cardboard box; *every day* they <u>are</u> only three feet tall.
5. George <u>sweated</u> profusely as he <u>dug</u> six holes in his yard.
    Every day George <u>sweats</u> profusely as he <u>digs</u> six holes in his yard.
6. Blisters <u>stung</u> his hands, yet he <u>continued</u> working.
    Every day Blisters <u>sting</u> his hands, yet he <u>continues</u> working.
7. Then he <u>shoveled</u> compost into each hole.
    Every day Then he <u>shovels</u> compost into each hole.
8. After planting the trees, George <u>firmed</u> the soil around their roots.
    Every day After planting the trees, George <u>firms</u> the soil around their roots.

9. Soon the little trees <u>will bloom</u>, and the blossoms <u>will look</u> so pretty.
   Yesterday Soon the little trees <u>bloomed</u>, and *yesterday* the blossoms <u>looked</u> so pretty.
10. In only four years, George <u>will harvest</u> his first apples.
    Yesterday In only four years, George <u>harvested</u> his first apples.

Exercise 1.2 Finding Verbs

1. Video games <u>are</u> a multi-billion-dollar industry.
   Yesterday Video games <u>were</u> a multi-billion-dollar industry.
2. Many people <u>think</u> that *Pong* <u>was</u> the first video game.
   Tomorrow many people <u>will think</u> that *Pong* <u>will be</u> the first video game.
3. *Pong* <u>comes</u> from the game of table tennis; in *Pong* players <u>slide</u> the paddles back and forth to hit the ball.
   Yesterday Pong <u>came</u> from the game of table tennis; in *Pong* players <u>slid</u> the paddles back and forth to hit the ball.
4. Although *Pong* <u>was</u> not the first video game, its success <u>took</u> the video game industry mainstream.
   Every day Although *Pong* <u>is</u> not the first video game, its success <u>takes</u> the video game industry mainstream.
5. Earlier video games <u>included</u> *Spacewar* and *Chase; Chase* <u>was</u> the first video game for television.
   Tomorrow Earlier video games <u>will include</u> *Spacewar* and *Chase; tomorrow Chase* <u>will be</u> the first video game for television.
6. Some teachers <u>use</u> computer games to teach their students.
   Yesterday Some teachers <u>used</u> computer games to teach their students.
7. Programs <u>allow</u> students to play a game after they <u>master</u> a new concept.
   Yesterday Programs <u>allowed</u> students to play a game *yesterday* after they <u>mastered</u> a new concept.

8. Typing programs <u>include</u> games to improve typing speed.
   Yesterday Typing programs <u>included</u> games to improve typing speed.
9. Some museums <u>use</u> video games as part of their displays such as the stock trading simulation game at the Chicago Board of Trade Museum.
   Yesterday Some museums <u>used</u> video games as part of their displays such as the stock trading simulation game at the Chicago Board of Trade Museum.
10. After finishing these sentences, you <u>will reward</u> yourself and <u>play</u> your favorite video game.
    Yesterday After finishing these sentences, *yesterday* you <u>rewarded</u> yourself and <u>played</u> your favorite video game.

Exercise 1.3 Finding Subjects

1. Professor Smith's literature <u>class</u> <u>will study</u> poetry.
   Yesterday Professor Smith's literature <u>class</u> <u>studied</u> poetry.
2. The <u>registrar</u> <u>spent</u> two days fixing the schedules after the college's computer <u>system</u> <u>crashed</u>.
   Every day The <u>registrar</u> <u>spends</u> two days fixing the schedules after the college's computer <u>system</u> <u>crashes</u>.
3. <u>England</u> <u>established</u> the first toll roads in 1269.
   Tomorrow <u>England</u> <u>will establish</u> the first toll roads in 1269.
4. Dylan's favorite breakfast <u>food</u> <u>is</u> cold pizza.
   Yesterday Dylan's favorite breakfast <u>food</u> <u>was</u> cold pizza.
5. <u>Consumers</u> in the United States <u>discard</u> nearly one hundred million cell phones annually.
   Yesterday <u>Consumers</u> in the United States <u>discarded</u> nearly one hundred million cell phones annually.
6. <u>Tiffany</u> and <u>Erika</u> <u>will work</u> at Burger King this summer; <u>Jasmine</u> <u>will serve</u> as a camp counsellor.
   Every day <u>Tiffany</u> and <u>Erika</u> <u>work</u> at Burger King this summer; *every day* <u>Jasmine</u> <u>serves</u> as a camp counselor.

7. <u>Sharing</u> an apartment <u>requires</u> compromise.
   Yesterday <u>Sharing</u> an apartment <u>required</u> compromise.
   (An apartment by itself doesn't require compromise; sharing requires compromise.)
8. Many <u>people</u> <u>use</u> the internet to reserve hotel rooms.
   Yesterday Many <u>people</u> <u>used</u> the internet to reserve hotel rooms.
9. <u>Germany</u> and <u>Japan</u> <u>recycle</u> more than eighty percent of the glass and paper in their countries.
   Tomorrow <u>Germany</u> and <u>Japan</u> <u>will recycle</u> more than eighty percent of the glass and paper in their countries.

Exercise 1.4 Finding Subjects

1. <u>Jeremy</u> <u>bought</u> a new phone last week.
   Every day <u>Jeremy</u> <u>buys</u> a new phone last week.
2. His old <u>phone</u> <u>dropped</u> calls.
   Every day His old <u>phone</u> <u>drops</u> calls.
3. <u>Melissa</u> and <u>Kari</u> <u>made</u> an inexpensive desk out of a wooden door and two small file cabinets.
   Every day <u>Melissa</u> and <u>Kari</u> <u>make</u> an inexpensive desk out of a wooden door and two small file cabinets.
4. <u>Friction</u> between the brake pads and the wheel rims on a bicycle <u>creates</u> a bicycle's braking action.
   Yesterday <u>Friction</u> between the brake pads and the wheel rims on a bicycle <u>created</u> a bicycle's braking action.
5. On the day before Christmas, <u>tape, scissors,</u> and wrapping <u>paper</u> <u>cluttered</u> the dining room table.
   Tomorrow On the day before Christmas, <u>tape, scissors,</u> and wrapping <u>paper</u> <u>will clutter</u> the dining room table.
6. <u>Alonzo</u> <u>finished</u> his calculus homework, and then <u>he</u> <u>started</u> his research paper on Napoleon.
   Tomorrow <u>Alonzo</u> <u>will finish</u> his calculus homework, and then *tomorrow* <u>he</u> <u>will start</u> his research paper on Napoleon.

7. In the 1960s <u>Eartha Kitt</u> and <u>Cesar Romero</u> <u>made</u> guest appearances on the *Batman* television series.
   Every day In the 1960s <u>Eartha Kitt</u> and <u>Cesar Romero</u> <u>make</u> guest appearances on the *Batman* television series.

8. <u>Chandra</u> and <u>Francis</u> <u>planned</u> to go shopping, but their car's <u>battery</u> <u>was</u> dead.
   Every day <u>Chandra</u> and <u>Francis</u> <u>plan</u> to go shopping, but their car's <u>battery</u> <u>is</u> dead.

9. After his <u>computer</u> <u>crashed</u>, <u>Joseph</u> <u>tried</u> writing his paper by hand.
   Tomorrow After his <u>computer</u> <u>crashes</u>, <u>Joseph</u> <u>will try</u> writing his paper by hand.

10. When <u>he</u> <u>got</u> a cramp in his hand, <u>Joseph</u> <u>went</u> next door and <u>borrowed</u> his neighbor's laptop.
    Tomorrow After <u>he</u> <u>gets</u> a cramp in his hand, *tomorrow* <u>Joseph</u> <u>will</u> <u>go</u> next door and <u>borrow</u> his neighbor's laptop.

Exercise 2.1 Identifying Clauses and Phrases

1. The bog <u>turtle</u> <u>is</u> the size of your palm   **C**
2. <u>Lives</u> in the soggy soil of wetlands   **Ph**
3. The Alabama beach mouse   **Ph**
4. <u>Makes</u> its home in grassy sand dunes   **Ph**
5. <u>Construction</u> <u>threatens</u> its habitat   **C**
6. Snow <u>monkeys</u> <u>are</u> native to Japan   **C**
7. <u>Live</u> farther north than any other monkey   **Ph**
8. Thick, soft fur for warmth   **Ph**
9. Snow <u>monkeys</u> <u>bathe</u> in the steaming water   **C**
10. Of Japan's natural hot springs   **Ph**

Exercise 2.2 Identifying Prepositional Phrases

1. <u>Josie</u> <u>got</u> lost (in the old building.)
2. The chess <u>club</u> <u>will meet</u> tomorrow (in the library.)

3. <u>Max</u> <u>opened</u> the heavy door, <u>walked</u> (down the hall,) <u>went</u> (into the Registrar's office,) <u>sat</u> (in a chair,) and <u>waited</u> his turn.
4. The <u>mouse</u> <u>dashed</u> out (of the cat's paws) and <u>escaped</u> (into the woods.)
5. <u>Carrie</u> <u>placed</u> her Hannah Montana CD collection (in the trunk) (in the attic) where <u>she</u> <u>kept</u> mementos (from her childhood.)
6. The <u>archeologist</u> <u>found</u> two vases (of pure silver) (beneath a heap) (of rubble.)
7. <u>Renee</u> <u>took</u> some yogurt out (of the refrigerator,) <u>checked</u> the expiration date, and <u>dropped</u> the yogurt (into the trash can.)
8. When the smoke <u>detector</u> (in the chemistry lab) <u>rang</u>, the <u>students</u> sitting (near the alarm) <u>jumped</u> (in their seats.)
9. The <u>Lamborghini</u> <u>sped</u> (around the curves) coming dangerously close (to the edge) (of the cliff.)
10. <u>Rene Descartes</u>, a mathematician (with considerable talent,) <u>invented</u> a branch (of mathematics) known (as analytical geometry.)

Exercise 2.3 Identifying Phrases, Independent Clauses, and Dependent Clauses

1.	Always <u>bite</u> me	**Ph**
2.	I <u>try</u> to kill them	**IC**
3.	<u>When</u> I <u>am</u> outside	**DC**
4.	<u>Drive</u> me crazy	**Ph**
5.	<u>While</u> I <u>mow</u> the grass	**DC**
6.	I <u>can't swat</u> them	**IC**
7.	<u>Because</u> I <u>have</u> to push the mower	**DC**
8.	<u>Before</u> I <u>go</u> outside	**DC**
9.	I <u>put</u> on bug repellent spray	**IC**
10.	To keep the mosquitos away	**Ph**

Exercise 2.4 Identifying Phrases, Independent Clauses, and Dependent Clauses

1. In the fifteenth and early sixteenth centuries	**Ph**
2. Since the Aztec society had a strict class structure	**DC**
3. At the top level of society	**Ph**
4. The nobles were all related to the emperor	**IC**
5. Although the nobles performed different jobs	**DC**
6. Such as judge, priest, or soldier	**Ph**
7. Middle-class people were called commoners	**IC**
8. Worked as farmers, merchants, and craftsmen	**Ph**
9. Slaves performed the hardest labor	**IC**
10. Since they were at the bottom of the social structure	**DC**

Exercise 2.5 Identifying Phrases, Independent Clauses, and Dependent Clauses

1. The new phone was too complicated	**IC**
2. For Johnna's mom to use	**Ph**
3. She gave the phone to Johnna	**IC**
4. When the phone bill came	**DC**
5. The bill was extremely high	**IC**
6. Because Johnna sent too many texts	**DC**
7. On the bus, during lunch, and even in class	**Ph**
8. To pay her mom back	**Ph**
9. Johnna found a job	**IC**
10. At the cell phone kiosk in the mall	**Ph**

Exercise 2.6 Identifying the Invisible *That*

1. For Valentine's day, Xavier knew that Gwendolyn wanted roses.
2. But he was so broke that he gave her freshly picked dandelions instead.
3. Gwendolyn was so disappointed that she began to cry.
4. Xavier thought that they were tears of joy that she shed.
5. Gwendolyn wished that Xavier was a little more romantic.

Exercise 3.1 Identifying Fragments

1. <u>Weighs</u> more than one hundred pounds.   F
2. Since its <u>teeth</u> <u>grow</u> continuously.   F
3. The <u>capybara</u> <u>chews</u> on tough grasses.   OK
4. To keep its teeth short.   F
5. <u>Capybaras</u> <u>live</u> near rivers, lakes, and swamps.   OK
6. In Central and South America.   F
7. <u>They</u> <u>are</u> excellent swimmers.   OK
8. Because <u>they</u> <u>have</u> webbing between their toes.   F
9. When <u>Capybaras</u> <u>are</u> alarmed.   F
10. <u>They</u> <u>make</u> a noise similar to a dog's bark.   OK

Exercise 3.2 Identifying Fragments

1. <u>Earthworms</u> <u>live</u> in all parts of the world.   OK
2. Except in the arctic and extremely dry regions.   F
3. <u>Although</u> <u>worms</u> in the tropics <u>grow</u> up to ten
   or eleven feet long.   F
4. Most <u>earthworms</u> <u>are</u> shorter.   OK
5. Usually one to two inches in length.   F
6. An <u>earthworm</u> <u>is</u> typically gray or reddish brown
   in color.   OK
7. Five tiny <u>hearts</u> <u>pump</u> the worm's blood.   OK
8. Because <u>earthworms</u> <u>are</u> responsible for aerating
   and mixing the soil.   F
9. <u>Earthworms</u> <u>are</u> vital to agriculture.   OK
10. As <u>Charles Darwin</u> <u>discovered</u> <u>when</u> <u>he</u>
   <u>studied</u> them.   F

Exercise 3.3 Identifying Fragments

1. The <u>British Invasion</u> <u>started</u> in 1964.   OK
2. <u>When</u> the <u>Beatles</u> <u>came</u> to America.   F
3. The <u>Rolling Stones</u> <u>arrived</u> next.   OK
4. <u>Mick Jagger</u> <u>was</u> the lead singer.   OK

5. In February of 1965.   **F**
6. <u>The Who</u> <u>led</u> the second wave of the Invasion.   **OK**
7. <u>After</u> <u>they</u> <u>recorded</u> the hit song "I Can't Explain."   **F**
8. Next The <u>Animals</u> and The <u>Hollies</u> <u>became</u> popular in
   the U.S.   **OK**
9. American rocker <u>Elvis Presley</u> <u>sold</u> lots of records
   in England.   **OK**
10. <u>Although</u> <u>he</u> never <u>performed</u> there.   **OK**

Exercise 3.4 Fixing Fragments

Bold type indicates the fragments which are now fixed. Remember that
there can be more than one way to fix a fragment. Where I have fixed the
Fragment in #4 by taking out the subordinating conjunction, you could
take out a period instead.

1. <u>Alex</u>, an African gray parrot, <u>was</u> thirty-one <u>when</u> <u>he</u> <u>died</u>. **For
   thirty out of his thirty-one years,** <u>he</u> <u>lived</u> in a research lab **at
   Brandeis University.**
2. Scientist <u>Irene Pepperberg</u> <u>taught</u> him to speak. <u>Pepperberg</u>
   <u>worked</u> with Alex to prove **that** <u>animals</u> <u>had</u> **intelligence.**
3. **When** <u>Pepperberg</u> <u>showed</u> **him two objects, like a green key and a
   green cup,** <u>Alex</u> <u>identified</u> the similarity by saying "color." **To show
   the difference between the two items,** <u>he</u> <u>spoke</u> the word "shape."
4. <u>Alex</u> also <u>counted</u> and <u>did</u> simple arithmetic. **<u>Alex</u> <u>died</u> in 2007.**
   <u>He</u> <u>had</u> <u>learned</u> to count to seven.
5. Alex's <u>accomplishments</u> <u>seem</u> incredible **because a parrot's** <u>brain</u>
   <u>is</u> **the size of a walnut.** <u>Irene Pepperberg</u> <u>proved</u> **that** <u>animals</u> <u>are</u>
   capable of higher-level thinking.

Exercise 3.5 Fixing Fragments

Bold type indicates the fragments which are now fixed. Remember that
there can be more than one way to fix a fragment. Where I have fixed the
fragment in #3 by taking out the subordinating conjuction, you could take
out the period instead.

1. Gold has always fascinated humans **because it is beautiful.** Craftsmen in Mesopotamia used gold to create jewelry **as early as 3000 B.C.E.**

2. Gold is valuable **because it is rare.** Throughout history, only about 160,000 tons of gold have been mined, **enough to fill two Olympic-sized swimming pools.**

3. Isaac Newton first created a standard price for gold. **Most countries stopped tying their currency to the gold standard long ago.** The United States maintained its gold standard until 1971.

4. Gold is usually found with other metals **such as mercury or copper.** Miners send the gold to smelters **for separating the gold from the other metals.**

5. **Although humans still want gold,** mining new gold has become more difficult **costing more and causing more damage to the environment.**

Exercise 3.6 Finding Comma Splices and Run-Ons

1. When Nero attended the gladiator games, the bright sun hurt his eyes.   OK

2. He wore glasses with green lenses, the lenses blocked some of the light.   CS

3. The magnifying glass came much later; it was invented around 1000 C.E.   OK

4. Reading with a magnifying glass was inconvenient a monk got an idea around 1285.   RO

5. He used a piece of wire to hold two small magnifying lenses in front of his eyes.   OK

6. The monk invented the first pair of glasses, and his idea became popular very quickly.   OK

7. Since glasses were expensive, only rich people bought them.   OK

8. Eventually, the price came down more people wore glasses.   RO

9. Leonardo da Vinci imagined contact lenses in 1508, contacts were finally invented in 1895.   CS

10. Today optometry is an important medical field most Americans wear glasses or contacts.   RO

Exercise 3.7 Fixing Comma Splices and Run-Ons

1. Dinosaurs are classified as reptiles because they were cold blooded. (F)
   Dinosaurs are classified as reptiles; they were cold blooded. (A)
2. While carnivorous dinosaurs typically had pointy teeth, an herbivore's teeth were flat. (E)
   Carnivorous dinosaurs typically had pointy teeth, but an herbivore's teeth were flat. (C)
3. Dinosaurs laid eggs; however, most mothers abandoned their nests. (B)
   Dinosaurs laid eggs, but most mothers abandoned their nests. (C)
4. Some dinosaurs have unusual features. Scientists are trying to figure out the purpose of those features. (D)
   Some dinosaurs have unusual features; scientists are trying to figure out the purpose of those features. (A)
5. Digging up dinosaur bones is only the beginning for paleontologists; the real challenge is assembling the skeleton.(A)
   Digging up dinosaur bones is only the beginning for paleontologists because the real challenge is assembling the skeleton. (F)
   Digging up dinosaur bones is only the beginning for paleontologists. The real challenge is assembling the skeleton. (D)

Exercise 3.8 Fixing Comma Splices and Run-Ons

1. Franklin was born in 1706; he had sixteen brothers and sisters. (A)
   Franklin was born in 1706, and he had sixteen brothers and sisters. (C)
2. Franklin wanted to be a writer, so he worked in his brother's printing shop. (C)
   Since Franklin wanted to be a writer, he worked in his brother's printing shop. (E)
3. He was born in Boston, but Franklin moved to Philadelphia. (C)

Although he was born in Boston, Franklin moved to Philadelphia.
(E)

4. In Philadelphia Franklin met and fell in love with Deborah; consequently, they got married. (B)
In Philadelphia Franklin met and fell in love with Deborah. They got married. (D)

5. He started a newspaper; it was called *The Pennsylvania Gazette.* (A)
He started a newspaper, and it was called *The Pennsylvania Gazette.* (C)

6. Because the paper was successful, Franklin became famous. (E)
The paper was successful; therefore, Franklin became famous. (B)

7. Franklin was also an inventor; he invented the wood stove. (A)
Franklin was also an inventor, and he invented the wood stove. (C)

8. He discovered that lightning is electricity; consequently, he invented the lightning rod. (B)
He discovered that lightning is electricity, and he invented the lightning rod. (C)

9. Franklin traveled to England; he advocated for better treatment of the American colonies. (A)
Franklin traveled to England where he advocated for better treatment of the American colonies. (F)

10. He signed the Declaration of Independence; he also signed the U.S. Constitution. (A)
He signed the Declaration of Independence. He also signed the U.S. Constitution. (D)

Exercise 3.9 Finding and Fixing Comma Splices and Run-Ons

*My corrections are in **bold**, but there could be many ways to fix the mistakes in these sentences.*

Oreo cookies are delicious, **and** people eat them in different ways. Some people eat the cookie in one bite, but other people nibble it slowly. Many children do the twist technique. They twist apart the two wafers, and they eat the cream filling first. When I was a kid, I ate the cream filling first. I left the chocolate wafers for my little brother; he was too young to know the difference. Today I like to dunk my Oreos in milk, but proper dunking requires skill. If you dunk for too long, the cookie falls apart in the glass of milk. Oreos were invented in 1912. For the first three years, consumers had a choice. They could get vanilla cream or lemon cream. Lemon cream was discontinued, so we had just the basic Oreo for many years. Then double stuff Oreos were invented, and they started an avalanche of new ideas for Oreos. Today consumers have many choices, but my favorite kind is still the original Oreos.

Exercise 4.1 Basic Commas

1. First we unloaded all the gear from our cars, and then we set up our tents. *(Job #2)*
2. Since we didn't have a shower, we washed in the river. *(Job #4)*
3. For dinner we caught some catfish in the river and fried them over the fire. *(None—This is just one clause because there is only one subject.)*
4. Fireflies, crickets, and frogs entertained us as we sat around a campfire. *(Job #1)*
5. We unpacked the marshmallows, chocolate bars, and graham crackers and made smores. *(Job #1)*
6. After our hands and mouths were thoroughly sticky, people began to head toward their tents to sleep. *(Job #4)*
7. Everyone was sleeping soundly when rain began to fall. *(No comma is needed since the dependent clause comes after the independent clause.)*
8. One minute the rain fell in a drizzle, and the next minute we were caught in a torrential downpour. *(Job #2)*
9. When the wind knocked over one tent, everyone started to reconsider the wisdom of camping. *(Job #4)*
10. Around two in the morning we decided to pack up our tents and drive to Missoula, Montana, to stay in the Motel 6. *(Job #3)*

Exercise 4.2 Basic Commas

1. On May 15, 2017, <u>we</u> <u>came</u> home from the grocery store to find <u>that</u> our pet <u>gerbil</u> <u>had</u> escaped from his cage. *(Job #3)*
2. <u>Leo</u> <u>had</u> chewed a hole in his cage, so <u>we</u> <u>closed</u> the front door to keep him from running outside. *(Job #2)*
3. <u>Since</u> <u>we</u> <u>couldn't</u> open the door, <u>we</u> <u>passed</u> the grocery bags in through an open window. *(Job #4)*
4. As soon <u>as</u> <u>we</u> <u>put</u> the groceries away, <u>we</u> <u>started</u> looking for Leo. *(Job #4)*
5. <u>We</u> <u>looked</u> under the couch, behind the dresser, and in the bathtub. *(Job #1)*
6. <u>We</u> even <u>looked</u> under all the dirty clothes on my brother's bedroom floor. *(None)*
7. <u>We</u> <u>didn't</u> find Leo, but <u>we</u> <u>found</u> three dimes, a marble, and a stale granola bar. *(Job #1)*
8. After several hours of searching, <u>we</u> <u>gave</u> up. *(Job #4)*
9. Before going to sleep, <u>we</u> <u>rigged</u> up a gerbil trap and <u>filled</u> it with sunflower seeds. *(Job #4)*
10. <u>We</u> <u>woke</u> up on May 16, 2017, to find Leo sleeping in the trap, and <u>we</u> <u>bought</u> him a stronger cage that same day. *(Job #3 and #2)*

Exercise 4.3 Advanced Commas

1. The noisy, excited kids crowded into the movie theater. *(Job #6)*
   *The adjectives **noisy** and **excited** are coordinate.*
2. That old blue car is good enough for driving to work. *(None)*
   *The adjectives **old** and **blue** are not coordinate.*
3. My mother, the lady in the pink suit, is the keynote speaker. *(Job #7)*
   *The words **the lady in the pink suit** are not necessary.*
4. People who live in glass houses shouldn't throw stones. *(None)*
   *The words **who live in glass houses** are needed in this sentence.*
5. Football players, therefore, spend a great deal of time in the weight room. *(Job #5)*

6. Dogs that bark all night long drive me crazy. *(None)*
   *The words **that bark all night long** are needed in this sentence.*
7. Domesticated dogs, which are descended from wolves, are good family pets. *(Job #7)*
   *The words **which are descended from wolves** are not needed.*
8. The landlord finally replaced the apartment's orange shag carpet. *(None)*
   *The adjectives **orange** and **shag** are not coordinate.*
9. The imitation paneling, however, will not be replaced until next year. *(Job #5)*
10. People who don't brush and floss have a much higher incidence of cavities. *(None)*
    *The words **who don't brush and floss** are needed in this sentence.*

Exercise 4.4 Advanced Commas

1. The patient walked into the cold, cramped waiting room. *(Job #6)*
   ***Cold** and **cramped** are coordinate.*
2. Abraham Lincoln, author of the Gettysburg Address, is considered one of America's greatest orators. *(Job #7)*
   The words in the middle are non-essential.
3. San Francisco, however, has a much cooler climate than Los Angeles. *(Job #5)*
4. The barista squirted heavy whipping cream onto the steaming vanilla latte. *(None)*
   ***Heavy** and **whipping** are not coordinate. **Steaming** and **vanilla** are not coordinate.*
5. Mary wore a long black gown to the long, boring opera. *(Job #6)*
   *The words **long** and **black** are not coordinate, but the words **long** and **boring** are coordinate.*
6. The granite counter tops, a last minute addition, sent the new house over budget. *(Job #7)*
   The words in the middle are non-essential.
7. Roberto scanned the bleachers of the school's gym for his girlfriend, Jasmine, and her friends. *(Job #7)*
   Assuming Roberto has only one girlfriend, her name is non-essential.

8. Consequently, the teacher suggested that Monica get an early start on writing her long, complicated research paper. *(Job #5 and #6)*
Long and **complicated** *are coordinate.*

9. The girl who brought a snake to school received two days of suspension. *(None)*
The words **who brought a snake to school** *are essential.*

10. The soft lights in the counselor's office, however, contrasted with her loud, bossy personality. *(Job #5 and #6)*
Loud and **bossy** *are coordinate.*

Exercise 4.5 Analyzing Comma Jobs

1. Benjamin Franklin was born in Boston, Massachusetts, but he later moved to Philadelphia, Pennsylvania. *(Job #3 and #2)*

2. Monkeys have tails, but gorillas do not have tails; they are both primates, however. *(Job #2 and #5)*

3. People who can't drive must take the bus, the train, or the subway. *(Job #1)*

4. While Gloria looked in the mirror, the hairdresser styled her long, beautiful hair. *(Job #4 and #6)*

5. Melissa's husband, Todd, likes to fish, hunt, and hike. *(Job #7 and #1)*

6. After hiking all day, Todd soaked his swollen, aching feet. *(Job #4 and #6)*

7. They met February 14, 2014, at a party, and they got married on February 14, 2015. *(Job #3 and #4)*

8. I had not planned to go out this evening; I could, however, be persuaded. *(Job #5)*

9. On the first day of kindergarten, Maria watched her eldest daughter, Katie, get on the school bus. *(Job #4 and #7)*

10. Daniel washed the car, mowed the grass, and trimmed the bushes; consequently, his muscles were sore that evening. *(Job #1 and #5)*

Exercise 5.1 Apostrophes

1. The announcer's voice echoed throughout the stadium.
   The announcer owns his voice.
2. The Beatles first appeared on Ed Sullivan's variety show on August 24, 1964.
   The Beatles don't own anything. Ed Sullivan owns his show.
3. Jack Parr—Ed Sullivan's main rival—had aired footage of the Beatles in January 1964.
   Ed Sullivan "owns" his rival. The Beatles don't own anything.
4. The professor's car was towed because it was parked in the students' lot.
   The professor owns his/her car; the students own the parking lot.
5. Sam's cat's favorite game is clawing the drapes.
   Sam owns the cat; the cat owns its favorite game. (This is assuming that Sam has only one cat.)
6. The name Matthew means "God's gift," while Samantha's meaning is "God heard us."
   God owns the gift. Samantha owns the meaning.
7. England has had six kings named George.
   The kings don't own anything.
8. "Let's review for the test," announced the professor's assistant.
   Let's *is a contraction of* ***let us****. The professor "owns" the assistant.*
9. Graphing calculators are essential for students in upper-level math classes.
   The calculators don't own anything. The students don't own anything. The classes don't own anything.
10. Even though Frances owned a car, she had to borrow her roommate's car for trips over five miles.
    No apostrophe is needed in ***Frances*** *because of the wording of the sentence. An apostrophe would be needed if the sentence said* ***Frances' car****. The roommate owns her car. Trips and miles don't own anything.*

Exercise 5.2 Apostrophes

1. The author's previous lectures had been wildly successful.
   The author owns her lectures.
2. Six hundred people purchased their tickets months in advance to reserve their spots. *None*
   The tickets don't own anything. The spots don't own anything.
3. Early in the morning, the auditorium's air conditioning units malfunctioned.
   The auditorium owns the air conditioner.
4. The program's producer called a repair crew.
   The program "owns" the producer.
5. When the repair techs arrived, they couldn't fix the air conditioners because they didn't have the right parts.
   Couldn't *and* ***didn't*** *are contractions. The air conditioners don't own anything. The parts don't own anything.*
6. Sweat dripped down the author's face as she began the lecture.
   The author owns her face.
7. Some paramedics arrived to treat a man who had fainted in the auditorium's stifling heat.
   The paramedics don't own anything. The auditorium owns the heat.
8. The author didn't want any lawsuits, so she stopped in the middle of the speech and asked the box office to refund the audience's money.
   Didn't *is a contraction. The audience owns its money.*
9. The people's impatience with the two employees trying to issue refunds created an even more unpleasant situation.
   The people own their impatience. The employees don't own anything. The refunds don't own anything.
10. When they left, everyone had experienced the author's message: global warming.
    The author owns her message.

Exercise 5.3 Plural Possessives

1. The **cats**' clawing pole is ragged. **more than one cat**
2. The **goose**'s honk was loud. **one goose**
3. The **student**'s work was correct. **one student**
4. The **women**'s restroom was crowded. **more than one woman**
5. The **birds**' nest was on a branch. **more than one bird**
6. The **squirrel**'s nest was in a tree. **one squirrel**
7. The **children**'s playroom was messy. **more than one child**
8. The **man**'s coat was warm. **one man**

Exercise 5.4 Capitalization

1. For Christmas Aunt Josephine gave my mother a poodle named Ruffles.
   *Here the word **mother** is not capitalized because her first name cannot replace the family title.*
2. Many American companies have factories in other countries; for example, some Texas Instruments calculators are made in Utrecht, Netherlands.
   *The words **companies** and **countries** are general.*
3. Next Monday school will end at 11:30 so that the teachers can meet with parents while Superintendent Toni Godwin meets with the administrators.
   *The words **teachers**, **parents**, and **administrators** are general. **Superintendent** is a title coming before the person's name.*
4. Vincent D'Onofrio plays Robert Goren, one of TV's most fascinating detectives; his partner, Alex Eames, played by Kathryn Erbe, has been called the Dr. Watson to Goren's Sherlock Holmes.
5. Many English words have Spanish origins, including alligator, plaza, and stampede.

Exercise 5.5 Capitalization

1. We will go to Grandma's house for dinner.
2. My grandma makes great Christmas cookies.
3. For Thanksgiving Mom always bakes pumpkin pie.
4. My dad loves Thanksgiving because he likes to eat.
5. Miss Dixon went to Tokyo on her vacation.
6. Most of the people in Israel are Jewish.
7. On Wednesdays I go to my Spanish class.
8. Columbus sailed to America with the Nina, the Pinta, and the Santa Maria.
9. Many Asian people live in San Francisco.
10. We could go to an Italian restaurant, a Mexican restaurant, or a French restaurant.

Exercise 5.6 Colons, Dashes, and Semi-Colons

1. The most popular sports in America are football, basketball, and baseball.
   *No additional punctuation is needed here. A colon after **are** would be incorrect because the words which follow it are needed to finish the idea.*
2. America's most popular sports—football, basketball, and baseball—are viewed by millions every year.
   The long pauses provided by dashes are appropriate to set off the list of sports.
3. As an executive assistant for marketing, Jaime has traveled to three major international cities this year: Lima, Peru; Sydney, Australia; and Rome, Italy.
   The colon comes at the end of an independent clause and introduces a list. The semi-colons are needed in this list because the items in the list include commas.
4. Hillside High's Brad Pitt—no relation to the famous actor—has three favorite teachers: Mr. Smith, Mrs. Wilkins, and Ms. Cassidy.

The dashes provide a long pause to set off the extra information in the middle of the sentence. The colon comes at the end of an independent clause and introduces a list.

5. The week before Christmas, the malls are packed with people buying gifts; the week after Christmas, the malls are packed with people returning gifts.
    This is the classic use of a semi-colon to separate two independent clauses.

6. My old car got twelve miles per gallon; my new car gets thirty.
    The semi-colon separates two independent clauses.

7. Stefan—a true coffee snob—will only drink Starbuck's espresso.
    The dashes provide long pauses around the extra material in the middle of this sentence.

8. Only one thing kept me from flying to Acapulco for spring break: I didn't have any money.
    A semi-colon would be ok in this sentence because there are two independent clauses. A colon is a better choice because it gives a dramatic introduction to the completion of the sentence.

9. Jan spent her spring break in Acapulco; she went to Aspen for Christmas.
    The semi-colon separates two independent clauses. A colon would not work well here because the second clause is not really a completion of the idea given in the first clause.

10. When you're buying real estate, only three things matter: location, location, and location.
    The colon comes at the end of an independent clause and introduces a list.

Exercise 6.1 Pronoun Case

1. The first place prize in the school's robot contest went to Eric and (**me**).
2. Cecilia and (**I**) took turns driving home for Spring Break.
3. Mark invited (**me**) to play golf with (**him**) and Julian.
4. (**She**) and Patty spent all day stripping wallpaper.

5. Be sure to call (**us**) as soon as you hear from (**them**).
6. (**He**) and (**she**) decided to go to Hawaii for their honeymoon.
7. I know that (**he**) and (**she**) will have a wonderful trip.
8. Martha is coming over this afternoon to help Emily and (**me**) clean out the attic.
9. Nothing could have prepared (**them**) for the surprise when (**they**) won the lottery.
10. On Thanksgiving (**we**) all go to Grandma's house to eat the wonderful meal (**she**) and Grandpa prepared.

Exercise 6.2 Pronoun Agreement

The antecedent is in bold type.

1. **Everybody** should pack (**his/her**) suitcase before going to breakfast.
2. **Sylvia and I** got an early start on (**our**) holiday shopping.
3. Both **Bill and Roger** installed satellite dishes on (**their**) roofs.
4. Neither Bill nor **Roger** fell off (**his**) roof.
5. **Two** of the boys forgot (**their**) backpack.
6. All **employees** must submit (**their**) expense reports by Friday.
7. **Someone** left (**her**) purse in the conference room.
8. Neither the professor nor the **students** could believe (**their**) eyes when the lab rat escaped.
9. **Anyone** who answers (**his/her**) cell phone during class will be counted absent.
10. **One** of the girls fell and skinned (**her**) knee.

Exercise 6.3 Pronoun Agreement

1. All **students** must pay (their) library fines by the end of the semester.
2. Both **Sheila and Cindy** got (their) hair done for graduation.
3. **One** of the students left (his/her) flash drive in the computer lab.
4. **Everyone** can pick up (his/her) paycheck on Friday.

5. **Someone** left (his) football helmet and pads in the locker room.
6. **Three** of the kids left (their) permission slips at home.
7. Both **Cody and Dustin** were late for (their) 8:00 classes.
8. Neither Cody nor **Dustin** heard (his) alarm clock.
9. **Anyone** who brings cookies to class will get extra credit on (his/her) quiz.
10. Either the coach or the **players** will tell the newscaster (their) thoughts about the game.

Exercise 6.4 Subject–Verb Agreement

The subject is underlined.

1. Jennifer and Nicole (meet) at the Suds-n-Bubbles Laundromat every Monday to wash their clothes.
2. Either Jennifer or Nicole (bring) magazines to read while the clothes are washing.
3. All of Aunt Sadie's prize rose bushes (were) covered with aphids.
4. One of the rose bushes (were) still blooming, however.
5. Neither the employees nor the manager (knows) how to install a new roll of paper into the cash register.
6. Red Lobster and Olive Garden (are) my favorite restaurants.
7. Neither Red Lobster nor Olive Garden (takes) reservations. *Match the verb to **Olive Garden** since this is the name closest to it.*
8. Olive Garden, one of the best Italian restaurants, (serves) great spaghetti.
9. Red Lobster, which has a huge tank full of lobsters, (offers) fresh seafood.
10. Both Red Lobster and Olive Garden (have) wonderful desserts.

Exercise 6.5 Subject–Verb Agreement

1. Megan and her friends (work) at Starbucks.
2. Either Megan or her friends (take) orders from the customers. *Match the verb to **friends** since this is the word closest to the verb.*

3. Neither Megan nor the other <u>employees</u> (want) to take out the trash.
   Match the verb to **employees** *since this is the word closest to the verb.*
4. <u>Megan</u>, the newest of the employees, (has) to do this nasty job.
5. The <u>dumpster</u>, which is in an alley full of trash cans, (smells) terrible.
6. <u>Jasmine</u>, one of Megan's co-workers, (gives) Megan a sympathetic smile.
7. Before Megan got hired, <u>Jasmine</u> (was) the one taking out the trash.
8. <u>Megan and her friends</u> (enjoy) preparing the drinks.
9. The <u>coffee and tea</u> (smell) wonderful.
10. <u>One</u> of Megan's favorite drinks (is) a skinny mocha.

Exercise 6.6 Using Irregular Verbs

Ask your teacher to check your answers to this exercise.

Exercise 6.7 Correcting Mistakes with Irregular Verbs

1. The dog **bit** the mail carrier.
2. He **has** grown so much since last year.
3. The catcher **threw** the ball to first base.
4. Jill **came** over for dinner last night.
5. They **have** taken too many breaks today. OR They **took** too many breaks today.
6. The batter **swung** at the ball but missed it.
7. Jamie and Max **have** gone to the movies. OR Jamie and Max **went** to the movies.
8. Mike **got** a ticket for speeding.
9. Bill **taught** his daughter to ride a bike.
10. The athletes **drank** lots of water to stay hydrated.

Exercise 6.8 Fixing Mistakes with the Verb TO BE

1. They **were** at the house.
2. She **is** a nurse.
3. You all **have been** watching TV for three hours. OR You all **were** watching TV for three hours.
4. I **am** too tired to mow the grass.
5. You **were** at work.
6. They **are** too noisy. OR They **are** being too noisy.
7. I **have** been waiting for an hour.
8. You **are** the best player on the team.
9. He **has** been working on the car. OR He **was** working on the car.
10. We **were** so glad to get home before the storm came.

Exercise 7.1 Misplaced and Dangling Modifiers

1. I loaned my wool sweater to Jackie with the red stripes.
   This is a misplaced modifier; it sounds like Jackie has red stripes.
   I loaned my wool sweater with the red stripes to Jackie.
   OR I loaned Jackie my wool sweater with the red stripes.
2. To save electricity, remember to always turn down the thermostat when you leave the house.
   This sentence has a split infinitive.
   To save electricity, always remember to turn down the thermostat when you leave the house.
   OR To save electricity, always turn down the thermostat when you leave the house.
3. The museum curator showed the new painting to the guests hanging on the wall.
   This is a misplaced modifier; it sounds like the guests are hanging on the wall.
   The museum curator showed the new painting hanging on the wall to the guests.
   OR The museum curator showed the guests the new painting hanging on the wall.

4. Walking quickly, the convenience store is about ten minutes away.
   This is a dangling modifier; there is nobody in the sentence to walk quickly.
   Walking quickly, you can reach the convenience store in about ten minutes.
   OR The convenience store is about ten minutes away if you walk quickly.

5. The doctor suggested a new treatment for my ingrown toenail that is painless.
   This is a misplaced modifier; it sounds like the ingrown toenail is painless.
   The doctor suggested a new, painless treatment for my ingrown toenail.
   OR For my ingrown toenail, the doctor suggested a new treatment that is painless.

6. Patrick promised to never leave the milk out overnight again.
   This is a split infinitive.
   Patrick promised never to leave the milk out overnight again.

7. Sara ordered a bagel from the waitress with cream cheese.
   This is a misplaced modifier. It sounds like the waitress had cream cheese.
   Sara ordered a bagel with cream cheese from the waitress.

8. Eating tacos, the salsa dripped all over my hands.
   This is a dangling modifier. Who is eating the tacos?
   When I was eating tacos, the salsa dripped all over my hands.

9. While studying for my history exam, my roommate turned on the tv.
   This is a dangling modifier. Who is studying? It sounds like the roommate is studying.
   While I was studying for my history exam, my roommate turned on the tv.

10. The dentist told Kevin to always floss his teeth.
    This is a split infinitive.
    The dentist told Kevin always to floss his teeth.
    OR The dentist told Kevin to floss his teeth every day.

Exercise 7.2 Passive Voice

1. Sandy ate the brownies.
2. Someone beheaded King Louis XVI in Paris in 1793.
3. George washed the dishes.
4. The pirate dug up the buried treasure chest.
5. A member of the committee released the incorrect statistics.
6. Someone found three priceless paintings in a storage unit.
7. The board approved the new construction project.
8. Someone had inspected the faulty valve two months earlier.
9. The ushers will take tickets.
10. Someone will release the new movie on October 1.

Exercise 7.3 Wordiness

This paragraph could be revised in many ways. Here is one example of a revision that eliminates the wordiness:

If a quick pull on the starting cord does not start the mower's engine, press the primer button several times and then try pulling the cord again.

Exercise 7.4 Parallel Structure

1. In the attic, I found a broken typewriter, an old suitcase, and a dusty doll house.
2. Scott was voted player of the year for his speed, concentration, and leadership.
3. Florida is a popular vacation spot because it has theme parks, beaches, and great weather.
4. Jan's new job pays well, has great benefits, and provides two weeks of vacation.

> *Other options are **gives** two weeks of vacation,*
> ***offers** two weeks of vacation, etc.*

5. The mouse ran across the kitchen floor, behind the refrigerator, and into a hole.

6. The movie was dramatic and exciting.
7. Patricia went to the grocery store, the dry cleaners, and the bank.
8. The library smelled like mildew, dust, and old books.
9. During spring break, Jake wants to go to the beach, eat lots of seafood, and get a tan.
10. The flight attendants were cheerful, friendly, and smiling.

Exercise 9.1 Analyzing Sentence Types

1. After Chelsea left, Jordan found himself bored and restless. **CX**
2. He spent several days watching TV and playing video games. **S**
3. Chelsea sent him pictures of the Globe Theatre and Big Ben, and he sent her pictures of his cactus and the empty basketball court. **CP**
4. One day Jordan walked the entire campus, discovering numerous new buildings. **S**
5. The next day he returned to the Career Center where he found job postings and internship opportunities. **CX**
6. Chelsea, meanwhile, sent pictures of the Eiffel Tower. **S**
7. When Jordan found a local company looking for an intern in their accounting department, he e-mailed to ask about the position; they immediately replied that they had a sudden opening. **CPX**
8. The previous intern left in disgrace after he spilled coffee on the computer. **CX**
9. Jordan spent the next six weeks as an intern. **S**
10. At the end of the summer, Chelsea had numerous adventures in Europe to share, and Jordan had an internship experience for his resume. **CP**

Exercise 9.2 Analyzing Sentence Types

1. Because they eat a lot of vegetation, elephants travel long distances. CX
2. In just one day, an average elephant will eat over three hundred pounds of vegetation. S

3. <u>Elephants</u> <u>grow</u> up to twelve feet tall, and <u>they</u> <u>weigh</u> up to fourteen hundred pounds. CP
4. <u>Elephants</u> <u>have</u> the largest brain of any animal; a typical elephant <u>brain</u> <u>is</u> four times as large as a human brain.
5. An elephant's <u>trunk</u> <u>is</u> very sensitive <u>because</u> <u>it</u> <u>contains</u> forty thousand muscles; an <u>elephant</u> <u>can</u> pick up a small coin with its trunk. CPX
6. <u>Although</u> <u>predators</u> <u>will kill</u> baby elephants, adult <u>elephants</u> <u>are</u> typically safe from all predators except humans. CX
7. Despite their reputation for never forgetting anything, an elephant's <u>memory</u> <u>is</u> similar to a cat's. S
8. The white elephant <u>gift</u> <u>originated</u> in ancient Asia <u>where</u> ordinary <u>elephants</u> <u>were</u> common, but white <u>elephants</u> <u>were</u> rare. CPX
9. <u>Since</u> white <u>elephants</u> <u>were</u> sacred, the unlucky <u>owner</u> of a white elephant <u>had</u> to feed it special food and <u>entertain</u> the elephant's many visitors. CX

> *Although this sentence has three verbs, it has only two subjects, so it is CX, not CPX.*

10. <u>No one</u> <u>wanted</u> to receive a white elephant as a gift. S

Exercise 9.3 Tricky Sentence Types

1. <u>Zork</u> and <u>Zink</u> <u>were</u> aliens from the planet Zigland. **S**
2. <u>Because</u> <u>they</u> <u>were</u> scientists, <u>they</u> <u>wanted</u> to visit Earth, so <u>they</u> <u>traveled</u> nearly a million miles. **CPX**
3. <u>When</u> <u>they</u> <u>landed</u> on Earth, <u>they</u> <u>were</u> astonished by the colors. **CX**
4. On Zigland the <u>grass</u> <u>is</u> purple, and the <u>sky</u> <u>looks</u> yellow. **CP**
5. After climbing down from their space ship, <u>Zork</u> and <u>Zink</u> <u>went</u> exploring. **S**
6. <u>They</u> <u>gathered</u> plant specimens and <u>took</u> water samples. **S**
7. <u>Although</u> <u>they</u> <u>wanted</u> to interview some animals, <u>they</u> <u>failed</u> to make sense of the animals' noises. **CX**

8. Since <u>Zork</u> and <u>Zink</u> <u>were</u> the size of mice, a stray <u>cat</u> <u>chased</u> and <u>cornered</u> them; <u>she</u> <u>hoped</u> for a new lunch meat. **CPX**
9. The tiny <u>scientists</u> immediately <u>beamed</u> themselves back to their ship and <u>took</u> off for Zigland. **S**
10. After returning to Zigland with their samples, <u>they</u> <u>received</u> a hero's welcome. **S**

Exercise 10.1 You will need to ask your teacher to check your paraphrasing practice.
Exercise 10.2 Answers are given in the text.
Exercise 10.3 You will need to ask your teacher to check your paraphrasing practice.
Exercise 10.4 You will need to ask your teacher to check your highlighting.
Exercise 10.5 Answers are given in the text.

Exercise 10.6 Works Cited Listings

1. Ehrenreich, Barbara. *Bait and Switch: The (Futile) Pursuit of the American Dream.* Metropolitan, 2005.
    In-Text Citation: (Ehrenreigh 25)*
            *any number for the page number is fine
    Signal Phrase: According to Ehrenreich
            OR Ehrenreich states that
            Etc.

2. Hamilton, Edith. *Mythology.* Little, Brown, 1942.
    In-Text Citation: (Hamilton 25)*
            *any number for the page number is fine
    Signal Phrase: According to Hamilton
            OR Hamilton points out that
            Etc.

3. "Colombus, Christopher." *The Columbia Encyclopedia,* 5th ed., Columbia UP, 1993.

    In-Text Citation: ("Colombus")

    Signal Phrase: According to the Columbia Encyclopedia

        Etc.

4. Edmonds, Patricia. "A Sleighful of Santas, Surveyed." *National Geographic,* Dec. 2016, p. 17.

    In-Text Citation: (Edmonds 17)

    Signal Phrase: According to Edmonds

        OR Edmonds writes

        Etc.

5. "Radioactivity in Drinking Water." *Mother Earth News,* Jan. 2017, p. 8.

    In-Text Citation: ("Radioactivity" 8)

    Signal Phrase: According to Mother Earth News

        OR Mother Earth News argues that

        Etc.

6. "Why Animal Rights?" *PETA,* 2016, www.peta.org/why-animal-rights/.

    In-Text Citation: ("Why")

    Signal Phrase: According to PETA

        OR PETA points out that

        Etc.

7. "John Lee Hooker." *Bio.,* A & E Television Networks, 2012, www.biography.com/people/john-lee-hooker-9343203.

    In-Text Citation: ("John")

    Signal Phrase: According to Bio

        OR Bio states that

        Etc.

Exercise 10.7 You will need to ask your teacher to check your highlighting.

Exercise 10.8 Works Cited Listings

Write a Works Cited listing and a parenthesis for each of these sources:

Winchester, Simon. *The Professor and the Madman.* Harper Collins, 1998.

(Winchester 88)

Halpin, Anne and Betty Mackey. *Cutting Gardens.* Simon and Shuster, 1993.

(Halpin and Mackey 58–60)

Wagner, Eric. "Way of the Wolverine." *Smithsonian*, Jan. 2012, pp. 13–15.

(Wagner 14)

Eligon, John. "In East Africa, Towns Suffer in Crackdown on Diamonds." *New York Times*, 6 Jan. 2012, p. A4+.

(Eligon A8)

"Election Chief will not Resign." *New York Times*, 6 Jan. 2012, p. A9.

("Election" A9)

"Man, Isle of." *The Columbia Encyclopedia.* 5th ed, Columbia UP, 1993.

("Man")

"Hummingbirds at Home: The Effect of Climate Change on Feeding Behavior." *Audubon,* National Audubon Society, 2014, www.audubon.org/content/hummingbirds-home-effects-climate-change-feeding-behavior.

("Hummingbirds")

Exercise 10.9 Reviewing What You've Learned

1. Accuracy, bias, and dates
2. Dates, place names, a person's name
3. Sentence structures
4. True
5. False
6. About one or two quotes per paragraph
7. Do a block quote—omit the quotation marks and indent the entire quote ten spaces
8. The reader would not know that you left some words out because your quote is a complete sentence
9. Square brackets [ ]
10. short
11. key word
12. in-text citation
13. True
14. You must put an in-text citation at the end of every sentence that includes a <u>quote</u> and at the end of each section of <u>paraphrased or summarized information.</u>
15. Page numbers

16. True
17. They both tell which source the quote or the information came from
18. In-text citations go at the end of the quote or information, and signal phrases go at the beginning of the quote or information.
19. Use an in-text citation to give the page number if the source has page numbers. Also use an in-text citation when needed to make it clear where the information from that source ends.

Index